IMPROBABLE LIFE

THE INSPIRING STORY OF HOWARD C. DILLAMAN

Don,
I trust you will be blessed + inspired by this book!
Michael

BY MICHAEL PEULER

An Improbable Life: The Inspiring Story of Howard C. Dillaman
by Michael Peuler

ISBN 978-1-63360-002-7
For Worldwide Distribution
Printed in the U.S.A.

Urban Press
P.O. Box 8882
Pittsburgh, PA 15221-0882
412.646.2780

Prologue

It's not where you start in life that matters most; it's where you finish! And God is up to the task of helping you finish well, no matter the obstacles you face throughout your journey. That reality was portrayed before me as I observed the life of my beloved father.

You could say that dad started life with one foot in a hole and the other on a banana peel. Like so many others in this broken world he quickly learned life had apparently dealt him a losing hand. Then he learned that no matter how bad things are, they can get worse! It must have felt as if the light at the end of the tunnel always proved to be the headlamp of an approaching train. He was perfectly positioned to have his life story listed under the already overcrowded category of "Tragedy." And to make matters worse, he had absolutely no knowledge of God.

But there are no unimportant or disposable people in this world. So even though dad had no knowledge of God, he would learn God had knowledge of him. He would learn it at the darkest moment of his life, when all appeared to be lost and his dreams of a brighter future seemed cruelly destroyed. He would learn it because of the quiet, rather unspectacular efforts of godly men; men who in faith placed Bibles in Veteran's hospitals. But ultimately he would learn it because of God's loving heart and God's pursuit of his soul.

I was born shortly after my father's life was immediately and radically transformed. You could say I was born in the aftermath of God's grace. For that reason, I quickly learned I had been dealt a winning hand. From birth I heard the good news of God. But just as importantly I witnessed the reality of God. Even when I foolishly ran from faith and boldly declared my desire to live free of the supposed restraints of faith, I never seriously doubted God's existence. It's hard (not impossible) to doubt God's existence when you're confronted daily with strong evidence that contradicts your doubts! As you've likely guessed by now my bold declarations proved to be rather empty ones. At age 19 I joined my father in following God. Looking back I believe his example was the single most vital factor in my decision. It's true, "More is caught than taught."

Dad taught me what it means to be a godly man and a godly father. I often think of his example as I deal with life's inevitable heartaches and disappointments. But dad did something else. From my birth he prayed that I would be called into pastoral ministry. And even though he wasn't aware of it, he taught me how to conduct myself once that call came. At the time of this writing I have spent 38 years in pastoral ministry. Looking back it's clear the truths that have served me best as I have served God and His church are the lessons I learned from observing my father. He taught me how to discern and follow the voice of God's Spirit. He showed me that the Spirit's leading is part of the normal Christian life. He taught me that God honors faith.

He taught me patience and grace and forgiveness. He taught me the freedoms and joys of humility. He demonstrated perseverance. He taught me how to die to self and love God's people even when God's people aren't loveable. And he taught me to see adversity as opportunity.

I want to thank my brother-in-law Michael for compiling this book. It truly was a labor of love on his part. As you read my father's story I pray you will confess Jesus as your Lord if you've never done that previously. If you're already following Jesus, I pray you will be drawn to see Him more clearly and to find and follow your purpose. If you're battling doubts, I pray dad's story will help you to trust God more deeply. If you're despairing, I pray God will replace your persistent despair with equally persistent hope. If things are dark in your life, I pray you will see the Light of the world in a new way. And finally, I want to remind you that this story is first and foremost our heavenly Father's story. It's the story of God intervening in a life seemingly destined for the scrap heap. It's a story that would never have been written if not for God's grace. Trust me when I say that dad wouldn't have wanted you to think otherwise.

Dr. Rockwell Dillaman
Pittsburgh, PA
November 2014

Introduction

I have been blessed throughout my life, in spite of my numerous missteps and mistakes. I had loving parents and a great childhood with caring siblings. Today I have two children and eight grandchildren. I had a successful career as a Certified Public accountant (CPA), Certified Financial Planner (CFP) and as a bank executive. I have visited 24 countries and have played some of the world's greatest golf courses. More importantly, two individuals outside my immediate family have touched my life in special ways. When I met them, I immediately had a sense that they were unique and had something I needed. For me, these folks were (and became with time) bigger than daily life. These two brought life into real focus, showing me that life is a purposeful journey and not just a period of time to simply exist or waste. They lived their lives in a way that showed me how it was to be lived. These two people were my accounting firm's founding partner, Simon Lever, who hired me in 1977, and my father-in-law, Howard C. Dillaman. Interestingly, one was Jewish and the other was a Christian, but both men were faithful to their faith and their families.

Simon Lever counseled and taught me how to conduct myself professionally. "Do it right – no cutting corners," he would say. He hated losing money on any accounting work but he would if it meant doing the job correctly. The reputation of his firm was that it was composed of high quality individuals who provided exceptional service and therefore, because of that culture of excellence, he attracted and developed quality partners and employees. After I left the firm to pursue opportunities in banking, we would still occasionally cross paths. The first words out of his mouth were never, "How's your career going?" or "How's business?" or "How much money are you making?" It was always, "How is your family?" Simon Lever ***always*** put family first.

When my wife and I applied to adopt a baby, he was the first person I asked for a reference. I knew he would be honest and that his opinion was respected in the community. I would learn over time the horrific challenges his family endured during World War II as Jews. The Holocaust was not a distant historical event for him – it was reality! Reflecting back, it was no wonder family meant so much to him. I always had great respect for him and his family and am thankful for the way he touched my life. I should have paid more attention to what he told me at various times in my life, but all in all he was a wonderful mentor and an even better person.

A number of years later I met the person who is the subject of this book, Howard C. Dillaman, who was known as "Papa" to his family (and how I will affectionately refer to him throughout the remainder of this book). He would eventually become my father-in-law but that had no bearing on my love or respect for him. It just allowed me to get closer to him, for which I am ever so thankful. I quickly learned that he was not just another person with whom I had a relationship. Every moment with Papa was special and full of wonder. As I studied and examined his life, I continued to be enthralled by his life journey and his faith in Jesus Christ. He was 85 years old and I was 55 when we first met.

Age provided no barriers in our relationship, but I must admit I enjoyed having an older man in my life when we met. My father and grandfather had died while I was young and then I lived many miles away from my immediate family. This relationship with Papa grew into a life-changing friendship and much more. Simon and Papa had experienced such difficult circumstances in their lives but yet showed me, by example, the way to live in spite of the problems. Papa's life was a classic illustration of how faith in Christ can direct and enhance anyone's life path. Papa talked and listened to the Lord daily and conducted his life in accordance with how he believed God wanted him to live and not how the world around him pressured or instructed him to live. Papa was absolutely sure of his salvation and his place in heaven, and that assurance was reflected in everything he did and even how he died.

I listened and watched him while he was alive and researched his life once he passed away. I came to understand and appreciate the transformation he had experienced. The more I researched and reflected on Papa's transformation, the more strongly I felt that I had to document it to preserve the story to encourage others and to remind the family just how special our heritage is because of this remarkable man. Jesus said in Matthew 16:24-25, "Whoever wants to be my disciple must deny themselves and take up their cross and follow me. For whoever wants to save their life will lose it, but whoever loses their life for me will find it." Papa did what those verses prescribed.

Papa may have been small in stature and devastated by his experience in World War II, but once he denied himself and followed Christ, God was true to His word and Papa found his life. It was a life that was quite truthfully an improbable one. As you read Papa's story, where he came from, what he suffered in the war and after he came home, I am sure you will agree that this book is aptly titled, for Papa's life ended up being both improbable and inspiring.

I want to tell his story because I know it will have the same impact on you that it had on me. Papa was one of those people who, once you met him and learned about him, had the power to change your life. You were never the same after you met Howard C. Dillaman – I know I wasn't. While God has a plan for all of our lives, sometimes we don't seem to understand or fulfill it. Papa clearly understood his calling and purpose and helped me understand mine. I hope this book will help you understand yours.

It wasn't always like that for Papa, as you will see. His life before Christ was in shambles. Yet Papa's remarkable transformation is another reason why I write. Like Papa you may also be facing tremendous pain and difficulties. Once you surrender to Christ, you can then also have as an improbable turnaround as he did. If God did a powerful work in Papa's life, He can do the same for you. And as He does that work in you, God can use you beyond your wildest dreams – just like He was able to with Papa.

For many years Papa had no idea who Jesus Christ was. He was as far away from God as a man could get. But once he allowed God to show His love for others and His redemptive love through him, Papa was well on his way to the abundant life that Jesus promised in John 10:10: "The thief comes only to steal and kill and destroy; I have come that they may have life, and have it to the full."

Matthew 28:19-20 shows that Jesus commanded His followers: "Therefore go and make disciples of all nations, baptizing them in the name of the Father and of the Son and of the Holy Spirit, and teaching them to obey everything I have commanded you. And surely I am with you always, to the very end of the age." That verse constitutes what is known in the church world as the Great Commission. Papa took this passage seriously. I saw it motivate him as if Jesus had said it to him in person. As a member of the Christian and Missionary Alliance (C&MA) denomination, Papa knew all about the Great Commission. He knew what God does to change lives because of how God had changed his life. Papa was not satisfied to let others make the effort to go and make disciples. He decided he was going to do all he could to make them, and you will read in this book just how much he was able to do with God's help.

I have never written a book but I have drawn on the Lord to assist me. Papa showed me that God takes us places we cannot imagine and that certainly applies in this situation. Philippians 4:13 states: "I can do all things through Christ which strengthened me." I had to trust in that truth whenever I felt inadequate or overwhelmed by the task at hand, and that happened just about every day! During this entire project Proverbs 3:6 has encouraged me with these words: "In all thy ways acknowledge him, and he shall direct thy paths." I trust God has guided me through this project and I hope this work will bring glory to God as I tell His servant's story.

Imagine if you focused on your calling, whatever that may be, determined to trust in the Lord to carry it out without fear and with abandon. That is what Papa did: he put his complete and total trust in his Lord. After he did, Papa touched thousands of lives and lived every day for the Lord. He understood that we were put on this earth to praise the Lord and model and live in God's saving grace. Yet, this all happened only after some traumatic events that changed his life. God was ***never*** part of Papa's life as he grew up or through his military years.

Before he gave his life to the Lord, Papa's mission was only day-by-day survival. Why did God protect Papa through those formative years? Why did God protect Papa during the war? He could have died like many others serving the country he loved. God had ***His*** plans for Papa's life just as He has His plan for you. I hope that you will ask yourself as you read this story, "What is my purpose? What is God's plan for my life? Am I living it?" After all, if God wants you to do His will – and of course He does – then He must reveal what His will is. Papa found it and never looked back once he did.

I want to show how Papa's life was changed, how he then helped change the lives of others and how you can change your life and the lives of others through Christ. Papa was a "disciple" of Jesus in the truest sense of the word. In biblical times, it was men like Papa who started out as simple fishermen or tax collectors, yet with the Spirit of the Lord working through and in them, they went out and proclaimed the gospel of Jesus Christ to an unbelieving world. It was said of those simple men, "These that have turned the world upside down have come hither also." (Acts 17:6) In some sense, Papa turned his world upside down as he walked out his faith just like those early apostles did.

Papa was not afraid to tell people that they must come to the Lord and he was not afraid to talk about hell. He was always armed with a Bible and as I studied his notes I found that he referred to three particular Bible passages. One was Matthew 13:40-42:

> "As the weeds are pulled up and burned in the fire, so it will be at the end of the age. The Son of Man will send out His angels, and they will weed out of His kingdom everything that causes sin, and all who are evil. They will throw them into the fiery furnace, where there will be weeping and gnashing of teeth."

Another was Mark 9:43: "If your hand causes you to sin, cut it off. It is better for you to enter life maimed, than with two hands, to go into hell, where the fire never goes out." Papa knew that we are not saved from hell by prayers, as important as they are, but only by the grace of God. Charles Spurgeon, the British preacher known as the "Prince of Preachers," spoke of the need to understand that grace transforms our hearts. Spurgeon said, "When I thought

God was hard, I found it easy to sin; but when I found God so kind, so good, so overflowing with compassion, I beat my breast to think I could ever have rebelled against One who loved me so and sought my good."[1]

The third and final verse is found in John 3:16 and is one that Papa constantly referred to with those to whom he witnessed: "For God so loved the world, that he gave his only begotten Son, that whosoever believeth in him should not perish but have everlasting life."

There are a few things you need to know before you begin reading Papa's story. First, Papa loved the King James Version of the Bible. It's not the most popular version today and it's sometimes difficult to follow since it uses archaic words. But that was the version that Papa used and loved and I felt I needed to stay true to his notes and speaking by using the Bible version that he used.

You will also find references throughout the book that God "spoke" to Papa. For some people that concept sounds strange and for some church people it sounds heretical! As I mentioned earlier, however, God reveals His will because He wants us to do His will. God is a great communicator and speaks through circumstances, through His Word and through other people – some who know Him and some who don't. Yet there do seem to be times when God speaks directly to people, and since the Spirit of God dwells in His people, this doesn't seem too farfetched.

In the Bible we see a story where God spoke to the prophet Elijah:

"And he said, 'Go forth, and stand upon the mount

> before the Lord.' And, behold, the Lord passed by, and a great and strong wind rent the mountains, and brake in pieces the rocks before the Lord; but the Lord was not in the wind: and after the wind an earthquake; but the Lord was not in the earthquake: and after the earthquake a fire; but the Lord was not in the fire: and after the fire a still small voice. And it was so, when Elijah heard it, that he wrapped his face in his mantle, and went out, and stood in the entering of the cave. And, behold, there came a voice unto him, and said, 'What doest thou here, Elijah?'" (1 Kings 19:11-13).

As you can see in that story, God spoke to Elijah in a still, small voice or gentle whisper. That was the experience of Papa. When you come to the stories where that communication happened, you judge the results for yourself to see if the Lord truly did 'speak' to Papa. In fact, there may be more times than you think that God is directly communicating with you.

Papa's improbable story is about a diminutive, broken man from a small town who was a giant for the Lord. His life was like yours and mine in many ways, and I trust you will find inspiration as I have in knowing that through it all Papa made a difference. The lesson of course is that if he did so can you. Papa discovered in life that you can't have a testimony until you have a test. I pray Papa's story will touch your life in a way that causes you to accept Jesus as your Savior and surrender your life, future and plans completely and totally to Him. If you already know the Lord, I pray you will utilize the remaining chapters of your life to spread the redeeming message of Jesus Christ.

And now, I invite you to read the improbable life story of one remarkable, inspiring man, my father-in-law and friend, Howard C. Dillaman. Let's not start at the beginning, however, but rather let's start at the end.

Part 1

Before The Lord

Chapter 1
Graduation to Glory

After living with his grandson's family for several years, Papa was almost exclusively confined to his bed as he reached the end of his life. While not in much pain, Papa was not accustomed to this quality of life. Papa's final days were near and the entire family knew it, including Papa. He was ready to hear the Lord say, "Well done, good and faithful servant, . . . enter thou into the joy of thy lord" (Matthew 25:23). He would peacefully lie in bed, glad for my visit as I held his hand. He was always grateful for the cake and ice cream my wife Victoria fed him and grateful for me (or any of the family) just being there. I never sensed he had any fear in those last days. He passed quietly on the evening of December 15, 2011 before the ambulance he was in had left the house.

At the hospital, as the immediate family gathered, I will always remember that there was great peace in the room where we were. What a comfort we all felt to have assurance that Papa was with the Lord. I have not always sensed that comfort when others have passed away, especially some of my relatives and friends who never knew the Lord. When they passed, we were all left with doubt concerning the destiny of their soul. Godly men and women have reminded and reassured me that if we have professed Jesus Christ as our Savior, our last breath on earth will be followed by our first breath in the presence of Jesus. What comfort we took that December night from knowing that our God was present in Papa's life right up to the end.

As a veteran, I was pleased when the family decided to honor Papa with a military funeral. The family was proud of Papa's heroism during his military service. He had kept his full Army dress uniform hanging in his closet and I know it would still fit him on the day he died. He retained many items from his Army days, including his duffel bag, a mess kit, his dog tags and a canteen. Papa was awarded numerous medals for his military service in England, Normandy and across Europe, with his service culminating with the Battle of the Bulge. They were all on display at his funeral home viewing, including his Good Conduct Medal, the American Theater Service Medal, EAME (European, African, Middle Eastern) Medal with four bronze stars, the Victory Medal, the Battle of the Bulge Medal and Outstanding Unit Citation Medal. Each bronze star on the EAME Medal related to his service in major battle campaigns. His uniform had a yellow Ruptured Duck Patch worn to allow him to travel at no cost on trains and buses while wearing his military uniform as he traveled home, even though he had been discharged from the Army. This was because military personnel had no civilian clothes in which to travel home. Papa's casket had the Army insignia on each corner and was draped in the American flag.

His viewings were attended by hundreds of people, many telling how Papa had led them to the Lord or how he had influenced their lives in some other way. As I observed his Army uniform and military honors there in the funeral home, I could not help but think of how close to death Papa had come in England, on Utah Beach at Normandy and in the rest of Europe. God knew Papa had sixty more years ahead of him to fulfill God's direction for his life – but Papa didn't know that at the time. What appeared so quiet and peaceful in that funeral home was really the joyous culmination of a tumultuous life filled with many events, successes, failures, friends, family and the like. I will relate many of those stories to you, including his military exploits, throughout this book.

Once Papa came to know the Lord, he realized how important every moment was. He taught me a sense of urgency so I would not waste the precious moments I still had to fulfill my purpose that would bring honor and glory to our Lord Jesus Christ. His viewing showed all who came his military medals, but his godly rewards were not displayed that day in the form of medals and uniforms. As I watched people come to the funeral home and speak to the family, I heard their comments and the message was loud and clear to me: "Michael, you have wasted many days. Life is not forever. Get it in gear for the Lord, *now* while you still have time!" I hope you are impressed with the same message as you read this account of Papa's life.

As with any passing, this was a challenging time for the family. We knew his days were short and his passing was no surprise. Yet Papa was always there for us and now he wasn't. It was the Christmas holiday season but Papa's passing was something that would impact us all through those holidays and ever since. We miss his presence, guidance, harmonica, smile and love!

His son, Rockwell, a Christian and Missionary Alliance Pastor, wrote the eulogy but was overcome with emotion, so he asked his son Jason to deliver it. It was a wonderful testament to Papa. Here was the message he read that day in its entirety:

A TRIBUTE TO HOWARD DILLAMAN FROM HIS FAMILY

In the early 1900s a missionary who'd spent over 30 years in Africa returned by ship to the United States. As the vessel approached New York harbor he spied a crowd gathered at the deck. A band was playing and banners were on display. He assumed the mission society had arranged a grand welcome home celebration. But the reception wasn't for him. It was for President Teddy Roosevelt – returning home from a safari. As his heart sank he asked, "Lord, why does a man returning from a safari receive such attention while I receive nothing?" In his spirit he heard the Lord respond, "Son, when you get home, I'll have a grand reception waiting for you. But heaven is your home, not New York! You aren't home yet!"

In this world where great attention is given to the passing of celebrities, most of God's heroes pass quietly, unnoticed by all but family and friends. But what goes unnoticed on earth is celebrated in heaven, a celebration this world can't imagine!

As a family we know that our father's reception in God's presence just days ago was something this world could never rival! Though small in stature, he was a spiritual giant. And while hardly a household name, he influenced hundreds of households. He leaves behind a legacy that includes:

- Courageous service to his country and a positive contribution to his community as a businessman with impeccable integrity.
- The eternal life of thousands he personally pointed towards faith in Jesus, including his three children, who passed that legacy to his grandchildren and great-grandchildren.
- The abundant fruit of a lifetime of service within and to God's church and anyone in need.

Dad loved and quoted the familiar tribute to Jesus entitled "One Solitary Life." So it is fitting that a solitary life that began in poverty in Coaltown, Pennsylvania, ended up influencing thousands. A child of the Great Depression who lacked a high school diploma, he made a great impact because he possessed his B.A. degree – **B**orn **A**gain by God's Spirit. And his legacy continues today through his believing family.

Dad left us powerful examples of unwavering love, consistent godly living, uncompromised obedience to God's Word, passion for God's Kingdom, fervent prayer, bold witness for Christ, humble service, tireless availability for God's work and often secret but never small generosity. Dad also leaves us with a storehouse of memories that range from the inspirational to the comical, including:

- The sound of his voice as he poured out his heart to God in his study to his favorite adjectives for those who proved despicable – "dirty, rotten pukes!"
- The perfectly pinned dress shirts, flawlessly knotted ties, always shined shoes and spotless vehicles along with the frayed top coats and the decades old wallet and Bible held together by black electrical tape.
- The unsolicited sermons on the virtues of buying sensible Chevys and Fords to the sudden appearance of a massive Lincoln Continental.
- The locked gun cabinet drawer containing large amounts of God's money to his protests that as a man living alone he needed only one plate, one glass and silverware for one.
- Fresh carrot juice and fish sandwiches for breakfast, the ever-present dried almonds and Little Debbie oatmeal crème cookies and the occasional piece of egg custard pie at the Venus Diner to the mandolin and harmonica versions of "It is Glory Just to Walk With Him."
- Stories of dramatic miracles and answered prayers to our own unanswered prayers when the fastest belt in the West was unleashed on us.
- Family Fourth of July's spent cleaning the family trailer at Camp Mahaffey to his predictable consternation on the trip home when we all couldn't keep it simple by

ordering the same exact sandwich at the drive-in.
- No television on Sundays to catching up on Sanford and Son and Bonanza four decades later; from Nana badgering him to spend a buck to new cars for all three kids when he won the big Electrolux drawing.
- His quiet, diligent service to our mother when disease made her bedfast in what were supposed to be the golden years to his stubborn refusal to ever let us know anything as to why he was suffering.

We didn't lose Dad last Thursday night. Someone isn't lost when you know exactly where he is! So today we sorrow but we also celebrate. We rejoice that Dad's trials are over. His often expressed desire has been fulfilled; he has seen Jesus, and his mother who died when he was only two. He's reconnected with Nana – our mother – his grandson Hilly, to Grandpa Fred – led to faith by Dad just days before his death at age 86 – to Uncle Lee who died in the trailer dad generously purchased for him, his brother Ron and the hundreds upon hundreds he led to Jesus who preceded him in graduation. Dad's favorite song was *No One Ever Cared For Me Like Jesus*. We have no doubt he has heard from Jesus, "Well done, good and faithful servant; enter into the joy of your Lord." And we can imagine Jesus presenting him with a golden harmonica for a rousing chorus of *It is Glory Just to Walk With Him!*

This message was powerful, generating plenty of both laughter and tears. One of the reasons for the tears may have been because we all wished we had done or said certain things to Papa and the opportunity was now gone. At times like that, we can be selfish in wanting something or someone we can no longer have. Papa was with Jesus and was no longer our companion or possession.

At the graveside, the local American Legion honored Papa with an honor guard and a bugler playing taps. Imagine how many times this scene has played out for our military veterans! A 21-gun salute was the final act to honor Papa. It was emotional for me, both as family member and as a veteran. The American Flag was folded by the World War II veterans and presented to Ian and Stacy Kingsley, Papa's grandson and wife, for their service as Papa's caregivers the previous four years. When that happened, we left the cemetery having had our final physical connection with Papa before he was buried. As we all left the question remained: How would we his family use what Papa taught us to continue the work of spreading the gospel as Papa had so passionately done?

I recently came across a letter my father wrote in 1970 after the sudden death of his father, Henry J. Peuler. My grandfather was only 67 years of age when he died suddenly of a heart attack while volunteering at church. The paramedics said he was gone before he hit the floor. Even though he was a Christian, my father questioned his faith for a moment. My dad, Maurice Peuler, sat down and wrote the following:

> If I only had five more minutes with my Dad. I have a whole lifetime of thanks to give him. He knows how I feel but I cannot tell him now. Dad left so suddenly – I

did not have that five minutes, I did not have the five seconds. God is great and I love him, but couldn't He have given me some warning? Couldn't He let me know that this was going to happen? After all, my dad was in good health and we had plans made. We were looking forward to many happy times. Maybe five years from now he would be gone but not now!

Five nights before a grandson was married, with another grandson to be married in two months. All the plans were completed. We had a different car to make the out of town trip and had taken extra odd jobs to pay for it all. He had given up vacation time, planning ahead for this trip. Everything was falling into place. We as humans had it all figured out. However, as we abruptly found out, God had plans also. Sometimes my plans do not agree with God's. Sometimes I can't understand – sometimes I won't understand. Sometimes I'm confused.

But I am not confused about this. My Dad is with his and my Lord. My dad has reached the ultimate. I thank God that my Dad helped me to know Christ. Christ was in my Dad. Christ shown through my Dad. Dad loved Mom and us kids. Dad loved people. Dad gave of himself. Dad trusted all. Dad forgave all. God has given us the grace to understand. God gives grace to those in mourning. God gives us eternal life. My Dad is with the Lord. 5 minutes. 5 seconds. I have things to do – **now!**

Isn't there a lesson from both Rock's and my father's comments? Your plan for your life is ***not your own!*** God has a perfect plan and he executes it as he sees fit according to His timing and terms. Remember, God does not make mistakes. Have you received our Lord's saving grace for your life? What are you waiting for? When you get around to it? Well, keep in mind that God's plan is the only plan with an exact schedule that is perfect and you don't know the time when that plan will come to an end. I urge you, I even beg you, not to wait. Accept Jesus as your Lord and Savior now.

And if you know the Lord, what is in your heart yet to do that you have not done? What are you waiting for? You are not guaranteed another day, let alone the years or decades you are counting on. As you will read, Papa made the most of every day once he gave his life to Jesus. That is part of his legacy, and I am writing this book to make it part of yours, too. The lesson from this book is: Make your life count for the Lord.

Papa's uniform and medals present at his last viewing

His viewing, the services and burial were an impressive balance of honor for a veteran and honor for a man of God! Papa's early life was difficult, even considered by some to be traumatic, as you are about to read. There was no mother in his home from the age of two, no God in his life, and an unbelieving father and extended family. There was the Depression, World War II and mental illness – all potential barriers to a successful life. But Papa rose above all of those barriers and lived an improbable life. I know as you read the full story to follow, you will also agree that it turned out to be an inspirational life.

Let's go back now and fill in the gaps of the story so you know for sure that this man in some ways was least likely to succeed and least likely to make an impact on a big world after his small beginnings. Let me take you back, now that you know the end to his beginning and chronicle some of the details that will let you know just how special this man was once he put his faith in Jesus. Along the way, I discovered some things about myself that I will share with you, some of which I was happy to learn and some of which I am ashamed.

The bugler at Papa's graveside service

Chapter 2
How I Got to Know Papa

Papa became an important part of my life when he gave permission for me to marry his daughter, Victoria, in December of 2006. I look back now and view it as a two-for-one deal in which I was the big winner. Victoria and I first met through an online dating service and, although we lived 250 miles apart, we bonded quickly. God overruled my plans and had different ideas when I placed a 50-mile limit on the distance I would travel to meet someone with the online service. Victoria's strong faith in Jesus Christ was important to me as I searched for a life partner. I had failed in a previous marriage and that failure depressed me. God put a marriage together and I helped break it apart. I had not always trusted God. I was proud, self-assured and content in every way. When I married again, I determined by God's grace that I would not allow it to fail. God needed to be first and foremost in my life and my new partner needed to share that priority.

Once we were married, I began spending a lot of time with Papa. He was always an interesting and intriguing man to talk to, especially when he talked about his military experiences. The wars in which we served were

25 years apart, but we had many things in common. It is my nature to talk a lot and I have always been inquisitive. I am always asking questions about people, their lives, personal feelings and the other things they've experienced. I believe that I am a better person for it as I learn from others. My times with Papa were amazing, informative and at times gut wrenching.

Papa became like a father to me in many ways and yet he was also very much like my grandfather. They were both wise men due to their life experiences and both men openly and boldly proclaimed their faith. I was raised in a conservative Christian family in western Michigan and the Lord Jesus Christ was always a part of my life in some way or another. I really never knew any other lifestyle. I had a couple of Catholic friends, had never met a Jew, a Muslim or a Buddhist and was not exposed to any other religions until I entered the military. My father, Maurice, was raised the same way by my grandparents, Henry and Alice Peuler, in the Reformed Church of America, a Bible-believing denomination. From its beginning in 1628 until 1819 it was the North American branch of the Dutch Reformed Church. It took its current name in 1867. Some of its most famous members were President Martin Van Buren and preacher Norman Vincent Peale.

I was raised in strict Dutch culture. My grandmother (last name Van Dyke) migrated from the Netherlands as a child. Sunday meant going to church, praising God, being quiet, taking a nap, visiting my grandparents and being reverent of God. I can still remember seeing people's shoes lined up on their front porch on Sundays while they napped. God forbid you worked on Sunday – even mowing your lawn or playing in the yard was forbidden. I was well acquainted with mid-week catechism, morning and evening church services on Sunday along with Sunday school, choir and youth group. I made a profession of my faith when I was sixteen, as much as it was the thing to do instead of from my heartfelt love for the Lord. When I look back, we were expected to make a profession of faith at an early age and that is what I did.

I wasted some college opportunities immediately after high school and left home at the age of nineteen to serve in the U.S. Air Force. Being raised in the 1960's was a unique experience. Your choices were college, working in a mill, marriage or the Vietnam War. Other than the three years when I returned home to secure my accounting degree at college, I never again resided near my siblings or parents. My grandfather passed away suddenly from a heart attack while I was home on leave when I was twenty years old. My father succumbed to cancer when I was 36. Thus, when I was asking Papa many life questions, it was as if I was asking both my father and grandfather the same questions. I regret not having such conversations with them.

Papa was patient and I know he enjoyed the times we talked as much as I did. As previously mentioned, Papa and I had one important thing in common – we were both military veterans. I am proud of my service to my country, including a tour in Southeast Asia during the Vietnam War, but I would never compare my service to Papa's. He was a great American soldier who served in World War II during the bombing of London, at the Normandy landing and at the Battle of the Bulge. He was a part of "The Greatest Generation" as news broadcaster Tom Brokaw had declared Papa's generation. I am in awe of his service to our country and often felt the reality and pain of war in his voice when we talked.

Once Victoria and I married and I relocated to the suburbs of Pittsburgh, Papa and I started having lunch every Tuesday in Butler, Pennsylvania at a local McDonald's. This is where I really came to know Papa. I mention the restaurant because Papa always said, "They have the best double cheeseburger." So we went there. Occasionally we would try another place but Papa was quick to say, "This isn't as good as McDonald's." When I ordered the burgers I would always ask Papa if he wanted French fries and his response was consistently, "No, just a coffee with cream." But I knew better. I would always buy an extra-large order of fries and spread them out on our table between us and we both ate them. He loved them but didn't want to spend the money on them! We would first pray and then get after that food.

Our conversation would turn to current events, family matters or something that was on our minds – we would just share our thoughts. If something was wrong in the family, he would listen to my report and say, "I know, I know." Then we would pray about it. I would come to learn that Papa did not like trouble or confrontation – it was too painful for him. His war experiences caused Papa to avoid conflict or tense situations. This was why he handled certain challenging matters in his life the way he did in later years, particularly matters concerning his children or his wife. I sensed Papa really did know what was going on but chose to pray about it and allow it to resolve itself. He was not going to confront someone or risk taking action when he did not know all the facts.

During those lunch gatherings I solicited his opinion on many topics. He was up-to-date on many issues even though he rarely watched television. In fact he probably had the only household in Butler County that did not have cable television. "Just a waste of money," he would say about it.

Papa was still living at home alone as his general health was quite good for the first 87 years of his life. He had a heart procedure in 1994 and later would need a pacemaker. Papa had high cholesterol and often the VA treated him for anxiety with various medications, but he was able to live alone with family monitoring.

Papa was always quick to remind me of a saying he told others, including his family: "If you are working for the Lord, the devil will constantly be at your heels." He would make a hand motion like one would shoo away a pet, "Get away, Satan, get away!" Papa was referring to Matthew 16:23 where Jesus said, "Get behind me, Satan. You are a stumbling block to me; you do not have in mind the things of God, but the things of men." Just like Jesus never stops strengthening us, Satan is relentless in looking for opportunities to weaken us. Over the years, Papa came to have a healthy respect for the devil's wiles, all the while putting his faith in Christ for protection.

Papa used numerous synonyms to speak of the devil in his conversations. As I grew up, I read some of those names in the Bible but Satan or the devil were usually the ones I had used. Papa knew his Bible and would speak of the "prince of the power of the air" and "father of all lies" in his ministry. It got me to think about all the other names used in the Bible for Satan. There are over forty, including "accuser, adversary, author of all sin, Beelzebub, chief of the demons, deceiver, dragon, enemy of righteousness, evil one, fallen angel, Lucifer, serpent and wicked one." I am sure Papa knew them all and he warned many people of Satan's evil ways. No one likes to talk about hell or the devil; they are not a pleasant topic.

There were numerous matters in our family in which the devil was trying to cause strife and Papa knew it. He reminded me, however, that we must put on our armor and keep up the fight. We are instructed in Ephesians 6:10-20:

> "Finally, my brethren, be strong in the Lord, and in the power of his might. Put on the whole armour of God, that you may be able to stand against the wiles of the devil. For we wrestle not against flesh and blood, but against principalities, against powers, against the rulers of the darkness of this world, against spiritual wickedness in high places. Wherefore take unto you the whole armour of God, that ye may be able to withstand in the evil day, and having done all, to stand. Stand therefore, having your loins girt about with truth, and having on the breastplate of righteousness; And your

feet shod with the preparation of the gospel of peace; Above all, taking the shield of faith, wherewith ye shall be able to quench all of the fiery darts of the wicked. And take the helmet of salvation, and the sword of the Spirit, which is the word of God: Praying always with all prayer and supplication in the Spirit, and watching thee unto with all perseverance and supplication for all saints; And for me, that utterance may be given unto me, that I may open my mouth boldly, to make known the mystery of the gospel, For which I am an ambassador in bonds; that therein I may speak boldly, as I ought to speak."

Papa knew how to activate and put on that armor and the means was prayer! Colossians 4:2 states; "Continue earnestly in prayer, being vigilant in it with thanksgiving." Prayer is our conversation with God. We are to pray frequently, glorifying Him, praying for others, making requests, being thankful and seeking guidance. We must use the armor God has given us! We know Satan's intention and must be alert to his ploys. It is through this alertness and armor that we resist satanic advances with confidence. This is what Papa taught, believed and how he lived, and I saw it firsthand.

We not only talked about spiritual matters, but all kinds of other topics including sports. Papa was not as much of a sports fan as I am but he would light up when the conversation came to the Pittsburgh Steelers. In Pittsburgh it is all about the Steelers. We also played golf a couple of times and, although he was in his eighties and had rarely played in many years, he was competitive. He was hard on himself when he would hit a bad shot. "Papa," I said, "you are doing just fine – you have not played in a long time." And his answer was, "I sure could do a lot better." It was fun to play with him but he was all business and just could not relax. I would later learn how competitive at work he was and how driven he had been most of his life. Papa and his family had struggled so much when he was young that once he was on his own, he was determined to make a better life.

Papa lived with his wife when I first met him in a simple home even though he could afford a larger and more lavish residence. That was not Papa's style. He understood that abundance is no excuse for waste – the abundance is for generosity. Papa lived his life like we are instructed in 1 Timothy 6:9-10 and 17-19:

> "But they that will be rich fall into temptation and a snare, and into many foolish and hurtful lusts, which drown men in destruction and perdition. For the love of money is the root of all evil; which while some coveted after, they have erred from the faith, and pierced themselves through with many sorrows. Charge them that are rich in this world, that they be not high minded, nor trust in uncertain riches, but in the living God, who giveth us richly all things to enjoy; That they do good, that they be rich in good works, ready to distribute, willing to communicate; Laying up in store for themselves a good foundation against the time to come, that they may lay hold on eternal life."

Papa's routine was simple – eat a healthy breakfast, go walk several miles at the mall, read the newspaper and his Bible and early to bed. He rarely watched television and if he did, it was the news or the likes of old television shows like *Gunsmoke* or *The Lawrence Welk Show.* He felt that certain food items (such as lettuce, tomatoes and peanut butter) were not good for him after he read articles in the newspaper or watched something on television that spoke negatively about them, so he eliminated them from his diet. His diet was quite limited and he was always conscious of what he ate. He had a juicer that he regularly used to mix carrots and celery to make a nasty drink he consumed at breakfast along with half of a banana. He also loved fish. His weight never varied – always around 130 pounds – just about what it was in the Army. This is how Papa lived his life until old age finally started to slow him down.

Papa, knowing I was a businessman, would inquire about my career and what I was working on at the time. The first time I showed him by business card he looked at it and then reached into his wallet to show me his from when he was a vacuum cleaner salesman. On it was the statement, "Christ died for you. What have you done for him?" Those two cards provided quite a contrast – my business card spoke about me but Papa's spoke about his Savior!

Papa would say things that surprised or caught me off guard. Once we were driving along the road and out of nowhere he said, "That just blows my mind – God always has. That just blows my mind!" I never thought I would hear an 87-year-old man say that anything blew his mind. There are endless lists of things about God that are amazing and beyond our comprehension. I laughed when I learned from the family that Papa would never swear but he would say "dirty rotten stinkin' pukes" when a person really upset him.

He was still driving when we first met but after taking a few mirrors off other vehicles, the family convinced him it was time to give it up. He kept a small revolver in the driver's side door and also had one in the headboard of his bed. Papa was at least a little concerned about security. I believe this was more a function of his upbringing during the Depression because he lived in a safe neighborhood. Papa displayed a "Guardian Security" sign outside his home although he did not subscribe for the service. His funniest trick was keeping a dog dish and chain at the front door, even though Papa did not have a dog! His mind was always working. As a young boy he had been taught how to pull off a trick or two. He still could as an adult.

Papa kept a few things in his dishwasher that weren't dishes, such as plastic grocery bags and aluminum foil, just in case they were needed. I often saw this same tendency with other folks who had lived through the Depression. They knew what it is like to lose everything so they often saved items that could be reused. I had a friend who owned a hardware store through the Depression and World War II. He told me that he sold a lot of steel pots and pans. When World War II commenced the folks that bought the steel items were encouraged to return them because the steel was needed in the war effort. The items came back in large quantities.

Papa's desk was covered with small note pads, used envelopes and index cards. There was writing on both sides of each piece, never wasting any space. His dresser drawers were full of these items, accumulations of more than 30 years of lay ministry. The notes included everything from scripture verses and names of churches where he had spoken to telephone numbers of old friends. His propensity to write everything down has proven to be extremely helpful as I used those notes to research this book. Papa did not like to waste anything.

Yet, some things never changed, like his wallets, sweaters and Bible. Papa's wallet was falling apart for years, but he would not change it even through someone would give him a new one every Christmas. On occasion, money fell out of it, but he just put the new ones into his dresser drawer and there they stayed. Papa's wallet contained so many things, from normal identification to a three-inch metal file for his nails. If you asked him to see or use it, he would hand it to you but he never took his eyes off of you until he got it back. He had it for many, many years. He carried a small laminated replica of his Army discharge papers and of course photos of his family. Fortunately Papa never owned a credit card so there was no security risk there. He did the same with the beautiful cardigan sweaters he was given; they just stayed in a dresser drawer or hung in a closet. He was comfortable with certain ones and had no need for another.

Because I had a lot of flexibility with my schedule I was fortunate to spend a great deal of one-on-one time with Papa, and we had many talks regarding his finances. Papa always knew where his money was invested and what is was being spent on. He had been an excellent saver. I know that surviving the Depression had a big impact on how he dealt with finances. He always had his checkbook in his pocket. Papa never used credit except for a real estate mortgage and those were paid off early. He paid cash for almost everything, including his automobiles. For most bigger ticket items he wrote a check. To say he was thrifty would be an understatement. One of the family's best financial stories about Papa was when his wife once stated her coat did not fit her and she needed a new one. He replied that there was no need for a new one. She just needed to lose weight and the existing one would fit again. Papa could be difficult to deal with at times, especially when it came to spending money.

Because he was self-employed all of his life as a salesman, he had to save for retirement for both he and his family. There was no company pension or corporate-sponsored 401(k) plan. He had to provide family health insurance, so he regularly contributed to an individual retirement account (IRA), purchased annuities and certificates of deposit and owned two rental properties. Spending during retirement was not something Papa did if he did not have to do so. He was content with his life and seemed to have no desire beyond the basic necessities. I wish I could say the same.

Bedtime was a great time to be around Papa and I learned to appreciate it when he stayed overnight at our home. He usually retired early, but just because he was going to his bedroom did not mean he was immediately going to sleep. I quickly learned that it was his time to talk to the Lord – and engage in a few rituals he developed over the years.

First, he always put his wallet and checkbook under his pillow. Then, he got on his knees at bedside. Papa, at home, had a long list of people he was praying for and he would pray for all of them daily. When spending the night at our home, the routine was the same without the list. I would get on my knees next to him. Praying was important to Papa as one learned while listening to his prayers. It was not just an exercise he did out of habit. It was a heartfelt conversation with his Savior. He was thankful and always seeking and trusting in God's direction. He was also humble, grateful and looking forward to the moment he would be with his Lord. He would be on his knees for 15-30 minutes before he went to sleep, thanking the Lord for his grace and love. He prayed for thousands over his lifetime. Papa saw prayer as a discipline and an act of sincere surrender before God, who sees our hearts. He prayed like he had just read Psalms 55:17, "Evening and morning, and at noon, will I pray, and cry aloud: and he shall hear my voice." Prayer is the means by which we can commune with God, praise Him, hear from Him and seek His direction in our lives. Jesus, in Matthew 6: 9-13, has given us a model (the Lord's Prayer) to offer when we pray:

> "Our Father which art in Heaven, Hallowed be thy name.
>
> Thy kingdom come. Thy will be done in earth, as it is in heaven.
>
> Give us this day our daily bread. And forgive us our

debts, as we forgive our debtors. And lead us not into temptation, but deliver us from evil:

For thine is the kingdom, and the power, and the glory, forever. Amen."

Papa wore his Bible out because he had read it and studied it so often. There was never a day that he was not immersed in his Bible and prayer. All of this came from a man who knew nothing about the Lord until he was in his early twenties. That represents an amazing, improbable and inspiring journey for a man who was left to guide himself at an early age but later led many to follow Jesus Christ.

Don't get me wrong – Papa was not a perfect man and he had, as you can already tell, many idiosyncrasies and quirks. I suppose we all do. Many of Papa's traits were developed through a tough life growing up. It is his stories of those formative years that made such a lasting impression on me. So let's continue our journey back to way before I knew Papa and continue to paint a picture of this man whom God used so mightily. As I tell the story, keep in mind I tell it in part to inspire and encourage you to rise above your past (or present) to be a champion for the Lord – just like Howard Dillaman was able to do.

Chapter 3
Childhood

Howard C. Dillaman (Papa) was born in the small town of Coaltown, Pennsylvania on January 4, 1920 to Fred and Sara (Wolford) Dillaman, who were 25 and 21 years of age, respectively. He was their second child, a small guy – weighing about 7 1/2 pounds at birth. His brother, Ron, was born two years earlier. Papa greatly loved his brother, who would one day marry and have five children. My wife, Victoria, related that she always had a great time visiting her uncle when all of the cousins could play together. Ron also was in sales but had many financial difficulties and Papa was always quick to assist him whenever he could.

Tragically, Papa's mother passed away during the birth of a third child (who was stillborn), leaving a young father to raise two young sons. Fred was a laborer at Pittsburgh Limestone Corporation and a taxidermist. Victoria also loved visiting his workshop, which had about every small animal on display, from snakes to deer. He possessed great skills and she adored the birds and the variety of animal specimens.

Papa's father was never exposed to the Lord or a church. Papa grew up in a manly world with no woman's touch of love or compassion. I believe this had a huge impact on his life in the ways he treated his wife, women in general and in his relationships. Papa was a tough, hard-working boy, always hoping to please his father. Like most children he had both the measles and chicken pox, but was generally healthy. He was an average student in school, but with the Depression putting incredible pressure on the family finances, he left school and went to work after the eleventh grade. I would say Papa got his advanced degree from the same school many men did in those days – the College of Hard Knocks. Many a person has had to survive by working hard. While slight in stature, he never shied away from hard work. He knew how tough life could be and accepted it.

At our weekly lunch meetings, Papa would share with me some great stories of when he grew up. One of his most popular stories involved a special chicken. The family rented a farm when Papa was a young boy for $5.00 a month. It was not an active farm but merely a place to live. There was no livestock of any kind, either on the farm or in the general area. One Thanksgiving Day the family was down to one piece of bread to eat. That in itself is hard to comprehend in our society today – three people and one piece of bread! How would you act or how would you feel in that situation?

Incredibly as Papa's father passed by the window on that Thanksgiving Day, he spied a chicken out in the backyard of the farm. Remember that this was not a working farm and there were no farm animals for miles. How did that chicken get to that farm? What did Papa's father do? Would he gamble the only food he had for his family and attempt to trap the chicken? That's exactly what he did.

Papa's father decided to build a trap and put the only piece of bread into it. As the chicken approached the box and took the bait they pulled a string and the chicken was trapped. Miraculously, God had provided a special meal for the family. To his dying day, Papa was convinced that God placed that chicken there to save the family and help them celebrate. The family did not know it then, Papa would say, but the Lord was watching over them. Only later would he truly understand what Jesus said in John 10:11, "I am the good shepherd: the good shepherd giveth his life for the sheep." There is no shepherd like Jesus. When we wander, He pursues us relentlessly. Even when we are not aware of His presence He cares for us.

Does God put things into your life that do not seem right at the time? Do you turn to God in those moments or do you just trust yourself and your own perspective? Papa shared this event to impress upon all who would listen that God still performs miracles and takes care of His children. Be mindful that Papa still knew nothing about the Lord at this point in his life. If you are a parent, you know how much you love your children and what you would do to protect them. God is the ultimate parent and takes care of His children in ways we are not aware.

The family had to learn how to survive and they were creative. Papa loved telling me how his father taught him to make counterfeit nickels in the basement of the farmhouse.

Papa as a young man

He would melt down old pieces of metal and make a pretty good nickel replica. Then he was sent to the country store on foot to purchase a loaf of bread, some milk or other needed items. I asked Papa, "Did the grocer know or even suspect the nickels were fake?" He would laugh and respond. "Maybe, but he knew we were poor and that he could just give them out as change to others."

"How else did you make money in the Depression, Papa?" I asked. He told me about how he had set up traps in local streams where he could earn a couple of bucks from muskrat hides, but the real excitement centered around his father's involvement in bootlegging. Papa's father learned from an acquaintance how to make the special brew and all of the action took place in the basement of the farmhouse. Vehicles or horseback riders came to the house to make their purchases – usually for a couple of dollars per quart container. One had to be an entrepreneur to survive back then. Papa related that it was not about breaking the law – it was about getting enough money to buy food to eat.

Papa was a young man and remember, he had no church training. It was not about right and wrong. It was about a meal. It was survival and Papa looked up to his father as a provider. Imagine how many cases just like that played out during the Depression. It is no wonder many of our senior citizens had such incredible memories of, and were scarred for life from, the Depression years.

Papa related a special instance where the "revenuers," as they were called, came to the front door of the farmhouse to verify rumors that they were bootlegging. Papa watched his father put his revolver on his side and off he went to meet them at the door. How did it end? Papa recalled hearing one of the "revenuers" say, "Look, he has a gun – everything must be okay here!" and off they went. This was the only time Papa could recall such authorities ever coming to the farm and he remembered that story with pride of what his father was willing to do to support them.

As a young man, Papa also worked as an automobile mechanic at a local gasoline station and he helped build local roads on a construction team. Trucks dumped a pile of large stones on the dirt surface of the new road and then the workers, with a sledgehammer, broke the stones into small pieces. A rolling machine then compressed the stones into the ground. Papa talked of how hard this physical work was but he was up to it. He recalled how many of the men quit. But while slight in stature, Howard kept working, sometimes teaching others how to break the stones efficiently. They were expected to break enough stones to make ten to twelve feet of new road each day to get paid, and Papa said he was not going to miss out on his payday. $5.00 a day wasn't a lot of money (it's the equivalent of $70.00 in 2014) but he earned it, helping his family survive.

Papa was born at the beginning of a special decade. The 1920s would be called the Roaring Twenties or the Jazz Age. Warren Harding was President and the American population was 106 million, as compared to 308.7 million in 2010. Vladimir Lenin and Benito Mussolini were coming to power and the large-scale diffusion and use of automobiles, telephones and electricity were significantly changing American culture. Albert Einstein was the most famous scientist alive. Louis Armstrong and Charlie Chaplin were among the great entertainers. The first commercial radio stations went on the air in 1920. Women were given the right to vote for the first time. Prohibition was the law. The most famous athlete was Babe Ruth. The Ku Klux Klan was growing in America. The stock market crashed on Black Tuesday, October 29, 1929, bringing devastation to many at the end of the decade. For Papa, the 1920s were a time of poverty and an uncertain future. While America was economically rebounding from World War I, Papa's family was entrenched in survival mode.

As I reflect on Papa's childhood, I cannot help but think of my own and contrast it with Papa's. I had two loving parents and four younger siblings. A sixth child was stillborn. We had food on the table three times a day, the utilities never went off and we had fairly new clothes. My father worked all shifts necessary in a Reynolds Aluminum factory for thirty years to provide for his family. Yes, we ate hot dogs and beans for some meals but most meals were balanced and hot. Being the first child and grandchild, I did not have to experience hand-me-downs like my younger brothers. I never had to endure the hardships Papa lived through as a child. The great country we have today was built on the backs of millions of people like Papa who fought to survive those challenging years.

Papa did take one major step in his young life which was to get married even though he was only 22 years of age. This relationship would be severely tested (and ultimately fail) as World War II engulfed America. It was this war that shaped Papa's life and future like no other event and set the stage for his improbable success. So let's move on from his formative years to examine Papa's experience during World War II and the years of the early 1940s.

Chapter 4
The World at War

I warn you that I am going to digress from our discussion of Papa from time to time in these next two chapters. I found so many fascinating side stories about World War II as I researched Papa's life and I feel compelled to share them with you. Having served in Vietnam, I can't help but contrast Papa's experience with mine. The differences are remarkable and I think worthy of your attention. Bear with me as we go through these history lessons together.

Also, much of what I include in these next two chapters is from my research and not from Papa's accounts. I found over the years that many World War II veterans were reticent and even refused to talk about the War. Their experiences so traumatized them that they could not bring themselves to talk about horrors seen and lives lost. I must admit that I thoroughly enjoyed the research but not the subject. War is not a pleasant topic and I realize that, while Papa survived, many had loved ones who did not. I cannot explain why one was spared, another wounded or maimed and still another died. As Papa would summarize his experience, "War is hell."

After the attack on Pearl Harbor in 1941, Papa knew it was only a matter of time before he would be involved in World War II. He did not relish the thought of going off to war, but he loved his country and decided he would serve if called. Keep in mind that no one knew how long the war would last or how long anyone would be away from home – or if they would come home at all. When I went into a combat zone during the Vietnam War, I knew my orders were for only 12-14 months. Papa, like the others, had no time schedule. The world was at war and they were not coming home until it was over.

My Uncle, Lawrence (Larry) Hilldore, served as a paratrooper in the U.S. Army in World War II, attaining the rank of corporal. He served in the 517th Parachute Regimental Combat Team, a unit that saw heavy fighting in Italy, Southern France and the Battle of the Bulge. Ironic that he was near Papa at the end of the war. I don't know why he became a paratrooper but many World War II veterans say it was for the additional $50.00 monthly salary (the equivalent of $687.00 in 2014). He was the only other member of my extended family to be involved in this war. He suffered injuries that caused him to lose the use of his right hand after being shot. He was awarded a purple heart and two bronze stars for his service.

I recall once asking him what was the most unusual thing to happen to him while serving. He related that he once parachuted at night into an unknown area. After retrieving his parachute, he took a short walk to relieve himself. He was surprised that he never heard anything hit the ground. He carefully returned to his original location and later discovered that he had urinated off a cliff! I have great respect for my uncle, who was a humble, Christian man. Once out of the Army, he served others, ultimately becoming the Director of Social Services for Ottawa County in Western Michigan. He cared a great deal for the disadvantaged and spent his life helping them.

On February 19, 1942, Papa, all 127 pounds of him, joined the Army with his first assignment to report to New Cumberland, Pennsylvania. Like the other soldiers at that time he was tough, having experienced the Depression and, in his case, raised without a mother and married as a young man. Upon completing basic training he was transferred to Fort Eustis, Virginia for additional training and on May 1, 1942 was sent to Camp Davis in Wilmington, North Carolina for specific skill training.

Through these trainings it was determined Papa had stereoscopic, or three-dimensional, vision. With this vision Papa could line up aircraft in the air with a stationary image on a telescopic device to determine firing objectives for an anti-aircraft gun. This was a unique ability that would determine Papa's path in World War II. Papa was the lead soldier on the M2 Height Finder, which because of its size required several men to operate and transport. While a typical rangefinder used a single eyepiece to locate targets, the stereoscopic rangefinders used two eyepieces and relied upon the operator's visual cortex to merge the two images into a single picture. To highlight how unique Papa's vision was, of the 15,717 soldiers who went through the special

Army Procurement and Training Program of ground combat troops between 1942 and 1944, only 920 completed the 12-week course for stereoscopic rangefinders.[2]

Papa at his stereoscopic Rangefinder

Papa told me on numerous occasions that he had no special abilities. But the Army disagreed and had him sent to a school where they found out that he had a most unique ability. Isn't it amazing that while we feel we lack abilities or skills, God has a plan that always is in place as our life evolves? Are you struggling with finding your special abilities or purpose in life? Have you trusted God to help you find your purpose in life? Have you even asked him to show you what it is? Papa used this special ability from God and served his country with great honor, though often at great peril.

Upon completing the intense training at Camp Davis, North Carolina, on August 3, 1942 he was promoted to Sergeant, the rank he maintained through most of the war. His gross pay was $97.50 per month (the equivalent of $1,365.00 in 2014). It would be only $153.40 per month almost three years later when he was discharged from the Army, although he did receive a $100.00 "mustering out" bonus upon discharge. This money was to provide funds for Papa to return home. He was then sent for training at Fort Sheridan in Highwood, Illinois, Camp McCoy in Sparta, Wisconsin and Camp Forest, Tennessee.

On April 19, 1943, Papa finally was ready for what was known as "Tennessee Maneuvers" in Nashville, Tennessee. These war games were held in the countryside because of the similarity of the terrain to Western Europe. On September 1, 1943, Papa was transferred to Fort Dix, New Jersey for staging to depart for Europe.

On October 20, 1943, Papa boarded the British Ship S.S. Monarch of Bermuda, a ship weighing 22,424 tons. It originally was a cruise ship when built in 1931 and part of the famous "Millionaire Ships," along with the Queen of Bermuda. Papa was one of the 6,000 men who arrived in Liverpool, England on November 3, 1943, having been part of a convoy that would transport 500,000 American soldiers toward the battle zone. After a brief stop at Kettering Airfield outside London, Papa was assigned to Bishop Stratford and Stansted Mountfitchet (both just North of London), where he would have his first contact with German aircraft. As part of the 405th AAA (Anti-Aircraft Artillery) Battalion, Battery B, they were attacked in 1944 by German buzz bombs on January 13, 15, 21, 22 and 29, February 4, 13, 19 and 23 and March 22nd that I can document from military records.[3]

As an example of how the AAA units were forced to respond to such attacks, the January 15th attack occurred at 7:50 pm (1950 hours military time) causing the unit to fire

18 rounds of 90mm shells at a single buzz bomb, which was traveling at an altitude of about 15,000 feet. On January 29th, seven buzz bombs were detonated with 387 rounds being fired against those rockets. Some of the attacks were from buzz bombs flying as low as 5,400 feet.[4] The V-1 flying bomb, also known as the Buzz Bomb or Doodlebug, was a pulse-jet-powered predecessor of the cruise missile. The V stood for "Vengeance." It was a radio-controlled pilotless aircraft that terrorized London for months in 1944. According to Stephen Ambrose of "Citizen Soldiers," London had 5,000 persons killed, 35,000 injured and 30,000 buildings destroyed by buzz bombs in the war.[5] They were launched from sites along the French and Dutch coasts. Once a V-1 crossed the English Channel, the defenders had only six minutes to bring it down. Later in the war, Papa would experience the V-2 Rocket, which was a short-range ballistic missile targeted specifically at London and Antwerp. It was no wonder Papa became a pack-a-day smoker in the military. Just the fear and tension would be enough to make one smoke!

After moving through Blandford Camp and Camp Cleeve, Papa was eventually transported from Langer Field, a major transport facility, to South Hampton along the coast south of London, to assist in protecting the major commercial port and industrial area. Papa knew then that he would soon be directly involved in the war in Europe. Normandy Beach and D-Day loomed on the horizon.

The D-Day invasion of occupied France was named "Operation Overlord" and occurred from June 6th until August 25th. Operation Overlord, in only 80 days, suffered 226,386 casualties with 36,976 Americans killed. For many soldiers, their rifle, an M1 carbine, was of little use to defend against the Germans. The weapon was just a semi-automatic rifle that used a fifteen-round clip and could fire 65 rounds per minute.

In times of war, there is a special bonding between soldiers. President John F. Kennedy once said, "No one has been barred on account of his race from fighting or dying for America, there are no white or colored signs on the foxholes or graveyards of battle." That bond is unique and special. Imagine the kinship between men like Papa as they approached Normandy Beach!

How did that bonding show itself? One unique way was by signing American currency as a unit. Have you ever heard of money that talks? Like the bill presented on the following page, they are called "Short-Snorters." A Short-Snorter is defined as "a piece of paper money upon which signatures were exchanged between those traveling together or meeting up at different events."[6] The one pictured in this chapter belonged to the father of Doug Sellers, a television producer at Cornerstone Television, a Christian television station in Wall, Pennsylvania. Doug tells me his father, Phillip Sellers, kept it with him at all times during the war. The bill contains the names of the men he served with on D-Day.

The name came from the slang for an alcoholic drink, often referred to as a "short snort." They have become popular collectibles since they are a unique record of historical events. This particular bill survived D-Day – something many men did not. Doug Sellers related that he was only aware of three times that his father ever spoke of the war in his lifetime. His father drove a barge transporting soldiers to the shore on D-Day, suffering shrapnel wounds during the battle. While traveling through Germany, he also had the unpleasant experience of coming face-to-face with an armed German soldier. For many years, he kept that German's belt buckle in his room in a shadow box, but eventually passed it on to a family member, since he did not want to look at the swastika on the buckle.

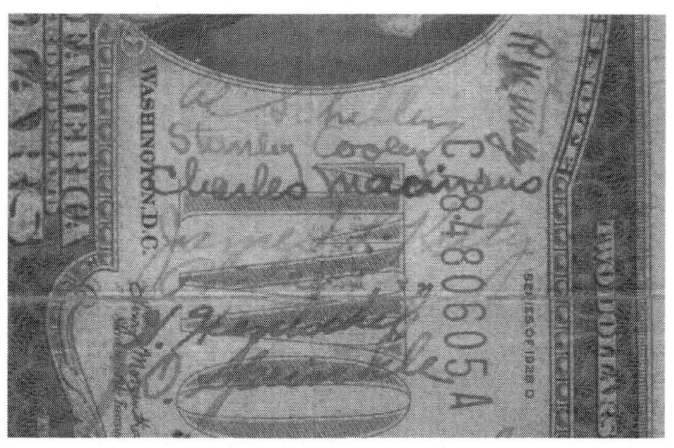

$2 Bill signed by comrades of
Machinist First Class Philip L. Sellers

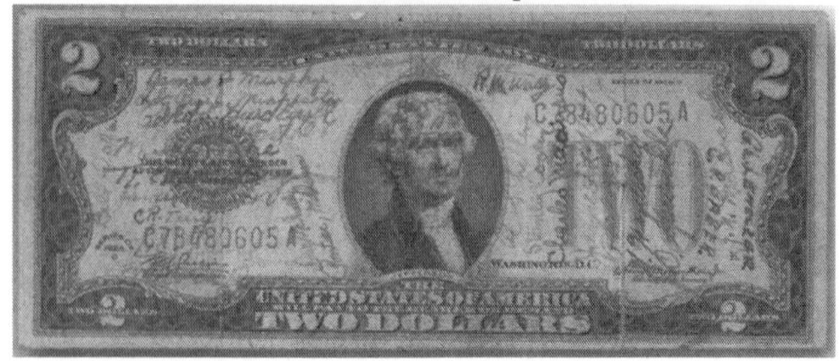

I found it interesting that Philip Sellers received a

letter from Secretary of the Navy, James Forrestal, upon his discharge. A soon as I hear the name Forrestal I think of Edward J. Wessels, a member of my church when I was growing up, who died in a terrible fire on the U.S.S. Forrestal in 1967 off the coast of Vietnam. A missile accidently fired on the deck, striking an aircraft piloted by now Arizona Senator John McCain. The subsequent explosions caused fuel to spill to lower decks where Ed was residing. The aircraft carrier had been named after the former Secretary of the Navy. I was just entering my senior year of high school and he was my first friend to die in the Vietnam War. It was hard to comprehend because Ed was a fine young man. The event really brought home the effects of war.

Within a week Papa boarded the "Prince Leopold," a British 2,938 ton transport originally built by the Belgians for Normandy. He arrived at Utah Beach on July 18, 1944. Was God still watching over Papa? Well, on July 29, 1944, (only 11 days later), the Prince Leopold was struck and sunk by a torpedo fired by a German U-261 VII type submarine.[7] Praise God that Papa was no longer aboard. God was continuing to protect his future servant!

While it was a short trip from England to Utah Beach, some trips took as long as five days due to unloading schedules. The signs of war were all around Papa from the events of D-Day, everything from sunken ships to wrecked amphibious landing craft. Occasional explosions from land mines could still be heard from the beach.[8] Having moved from the Leopold to a Landing Ship Tank (LST), Papa, along with many of his comrades, crawled over the side of the ship on a rope ladder with full field gear, duffle bag and rifle on his back. Into the ocean to an uncertain future they went. Unable to swim, he must have been terrified! Germans were heavily bunkered on an adjourning hill as he approached the beach. Bobbing up and down, Papa pushed on to shore. How does anyone survive this scenario? Thousands of men experienced this and it was only through the grace of God that they survived. Papa did not know his Savior at this point in his life but he would later tell the family and me that, looking back, God obviously had more in store for his life than dying on a beach in France.

Along with soldiers from other LSTs, he finally made it to shore, realizing that the Germans were still entrenched in a hillside-fortified bunker, pinning them down. After hours of fighting, several American soldiers were able to get behind the German bunker where, Papa related, it took flamethrowers to stop the German machine guns. These were some of the days that would become famous to the world in books, documentaries and cinema. But to Papa and many other veterans it was a haunting reality of the horrors of that landing. So many had died during the previous 60 days during a time of great bravery and terror. Now the next step would be a long journey across Europe.

After landing and surviving the deadly and terrifying sights at Utah Beach, Papa's Battalion moved toward Sainte-Mère-Église, France, about 20 kilometers (12 miles) from the beach. Using their stereoscopic radar and AAA weapons to bring down enemy aircraft, they arrived on July 20, 1944. Papa would experience the constant pounding of anti-aircraft fire throughout the war and eventually it would impact his health later in life. Remember that no one was being diagnosed with post-traumatic stress syndrome then and many others had the same experience as Papa. They were sent home after the war and had to learn to live with their battle stress as best they could. The sound of artillery pounding would follow and haunt Papa the rest of his life.

Papa was separated from his original battalion as was common for other AAA battalions in Europe who were never attached permanently to any parent unit. All anti-aircraft units were "separate" or "independent" battalions.[9] There were many different types of "independent" battalions since there were several different types of anti-aircraft artillery. They were "independent" because they were not an official part of a larger formation. (Sometimes they were called "bastard battalions," having no parent unit.)

U.S. infantry regiments and divisions had no AAA in them. The AAA units were assigned to higher HQ (Headquarters), such as a corp or a field army, and were sometimes called "corps troops" or "army troops." The idea was that HQ could move these independent battalions around as needed to supplement the divisions. In practice, these AAA units were usually attached to a division, more or less permanently. The primary U.S. anti-aircraft weapon, the 90 mm cannon, was used to attack high-flying aircraft. The AAA units were also intended to guard against low-flying aircraft with weapons usually mounted on half-tracks. Two other main AAA weapons were 105 mm and 155 mm guns.

The German Blitzkrieg in Europe forced the

widespread reevaluation of the Army's AAA capacity and in 1940-1941 a vast expansion began. On September 30, 1942, it was proposed that 811 AAA battalions be organized (with a total strength of 619,000 men). This large buildup became mostly redundant as the war proceeded and by December 31, 1944, there were only 347 AAA battalions with 257,000 men active in the Army.[10]

Papa manning the guns as he proceeded across Europe

Papa would eventually join the 6905th Provisional Trucking Company and the Red Ball Express near Sainte-Mère-Église and Utah Beach on September 16, 1944. The Allies had already landed more than 175,000 troops at that point and needed a huge supply capability to help move the battle forward. Given a common name in the express trucking industry, the Red Ball Express would operate 24 hours a day on a designated two-lane, one-way road reserved exclusively for the trucks, totaling 600 miles at its peak. The northern route was closed to all traffic except convoys delivering supplies, while the southern route was closed to all except returning trucks. Commencing on August 25, 1944, the Red Ball Express began with 67 truck companies; 3,358 trucks carrying 4.2 tons of supplies. Just four days later, the Red Ball Express included 132 truck companies and 5,958 vehicles.[11]

Keep that Red Ball Express rolling!

What is most often overlooked about the Red Ball Express operation in Europe was the contribution made by the African American soldiers assigned to Quartermaster and Transportation Corps units. Although three-fourths of Red Ball drivers were African American and African Americans manned a majority of the quartermaster truck companies, African American troops represented less than 10% of all military personnel in World War II. When the call went out to form the Red Ball Express, African American troops, in large measure, kept the supply lines rolling. The Red Ball Express has been referred to by some as "The Road to Civil Rights."

Drivers in convoy were instructed to maintain 60-yard intervals to present less of a target for the German bombers and a top speed of 25 miles per hour for safe operation. Passing was not allowed and no headlights were allowed at night. Allied reconstruction of the French railroad brought the Red Ball Express to an end on November 16, 1944.[12] Papa remained near the Red Ball Express to protect it until he arrived in Paris in November of 1944. He either walked or jumped a ride on a Jeep or a truck, which were constantly bogged down in soupy mud. The military might of the enemy was formidable and fighting the horrific weather made the endeavor even more challenging. Some trucks were sunk up to their axles and the men up to their ankles, according to James Alban.[13]

Everyone knows how common Jeeps were in the military. Almost every photo or news story involved a Jeep. Papa was going off to the military and the American

Bantam Car Company, in his eventual hometown of Butler, Pennsylvania, was one of the two companies being considered to build Jeeps for the U.S. Army in 1940-41. Ultimately, Bantam could not meet the Army's production demands of 75 vehicles per day at a specific weight. Thus, the Army gave Ford and Willy's the Bantam blueprint and they produced the vehicles the Army required. They fulfilled the Army's contracts for 600,000 Jeeps for World War II. I find it ironic that vehicles Papa used in the War could have been produced right near where he was raised and would eventually reside.

Papa in his Jeep

Commencing in 2011, a Bantam Jeep Heritage Festival, sponsored by the local Butler County Tourism and Convention Bureau, has been held in Butler, Pennsylvania. By 2013, the event attracted 1,557 Jeeps and 30,000 enthusiasts. World War II reenactments and encampments along with vehicle displays are just a few of the interesting activities still happening today.

During the long course of the war, imagine progressing either on foot or by truck, proceeding through numerous small towns. Many of those towns would be empty and others would have residents surviving any way they could. Many times these residents would reach out and assist the soldiers as an expression of thanks for their liberating efforts. Frank Alban recalls walking into Paris to the sounds of "Vive les Americans!" and "Hello!"[14]

Whenever Papa talked about France and Paris in particular, he would always say, "Denise Lagè, 16 Rue De la Paix, Paris." The family would often hear Papa say this but we never really gave a lot of thought to this comment. No one ever asked Papa why he said it. Why was this name important to Papa? How could he always remember this address in France when he could not remember so many other things? The Rue De La Paix is now a fashionable shopping street in the center of Paris. I believe this "Denise Lagè" was someone who truly helped solders, including Papa, as he proceeded to the war front in Belgium. Papa thought so much of this individual that he would eventually name one of his daughters Denise. Coincidence? Maybe or maybe not! We will never know because I never took the opportunity to ask him!

Papa would continue across Europe, in the heat and cold, experiencing the devastating effects of the War all along the way. No doubt Papa, like countless others, witnessed horrifying aspects of the war. Death, even in war, is a terrible experience for any soldier and it is combined with fear, loneliness and the extreme weather. Yet of all of

Papa's experiences he shared with me, one stood out from all of the others. As a small group of his unit crossed into a small town whose name he could not remember, they observed one of Field Marshall Gerd von Rundstedt's famous units. Those German soldiers had just taken control of this city. Papa, hiding nearby, watched as approximately a dozen American soldiers surrendered to the enemy tanks. As the men stood motionless before the Germans, suddenly the tanks turrets turned and mowed down all of the surrendering American soldiers. I can still recall Papa saying, "I hate that Rundstedt!"

Numerous accounts have been given of the killing of defenseless soldiers in Europe. Investigations and the famous Malmedy trials were eventually convened, convicting Germans of war crimes.[15] The trial of Col. Joachim Peiper's SS Panzer unit was held in Dachau, Germany. In 1999, I visited the concentration camp in Dachau and, quite frankly, it was an overwhelming experience. To see the remaining structures and being aware of what had taken place there actually made me ill.

The devastation as Papa crossed into Germany

Rounding up prisoners of war

From his landing in Normandy to his final battles in Brasschaat, Belgium near Antwerp, Papa traveled over 600 miles by foot or truck, serving with various units. Papa was able to rejoin his original unit, the 405th AAA, at Putte, Belgium on November 13, 1944, having traveled often with the Red Ball express and other units. From there, Papa's unit moved on December 31 to Brasschaat, Belgium, where they assisted in defending Antwerp during The Battle of the Bulge. While in Putte and Brasschaat, Papa's unit shot down 229 Buzz bombs through March 22, 1945.

Antwerp was a critical Port to provide supplies to the Allied troops, capable of receiving 90,000 tons of freight per day and was located hundreds of miles closer to the Allied lines than any other port. The Antwerp docks were within 30 miles of wharves, 632 operating hoists, 186 acres of covered shed space and oil storage facilities capable of handling over a hundred million gallons of fuel.[16]

Germans attacked Antwerp day and night for 154 days using buzz bombs. More than 5,000 of those flying bombs were launched toward Antwerp in a belated German attempt to deny this vital port to the Allies. It was said that the V-1 was eight times harder to "kill" than any ordinary plane flying the same course. These bombs were capable of traveling more then 360 miles per hour carrying warheads weighing just over 2,000 lbs.[17]

On September 23, 1944, General Eisenhower wrote to General Marshall, Chief of Staff, "Right now our prospects are tied up closely with our success in capturing the approaches to Antwerp. If we can only get to using Antwerp it will have the effect of a blood transfusion."[18] Later in the same report, General Marshall went on to say, "With the promise of a large increase of supplies through the Port of Antwerp in late November, General Eisenhower in mid-November launched a changing offensive to penetrate the Siegfried Line."[19] The Siegfried Line was a military front protecting the Third Reich with concrete bunkers, pillboxes, anti-tank ditches and minefields.

As stated earlier, there was no coming home for Papa until the war was over, he was wounded or dead. Having been through so much, little did he know, along with many of his comrades, that perhaps the greatest challenge of the war loomed on the horizon. The great battle ahead was the largest operation ever undertaken by the American Army and the fate of the battle hung in the balance for many days. Let's take a look now at what history has come to know as the Battle of the Bulge and Papa's role in it.

Chapter 5
One More Battle Before Home

The Battle of the Bulge was one of the most brutal battles of any war in history. John R. Bruning referred to it as the single largest battle ever fought by the United States Army.[20] It required more men, vehicles, supplies, equipment, aircraft and effort than any other battle. Even more than Gettysburg or the landing at Normandy. Thirty-one American divisions – a full third of the U. S. Army deployed during World War II – saw action in this thirty-nine-day battle. It would cost 19,000 American lives and cause 89,000 casualties.

Lasting from December 16, 1944 through January 25, 1945, the Battle was given the description as the Allied front line "bulged" inward on wartime maps. The Battle was militarily defined as the Ardennes Counteroffensive, which included the German drive and the American effort to contain and ultimately defeat it. It took place in the Ardennes Mountains of Belgium, France and Luxembourg. Germany hoped to protect the Siegfried Line by committing 250,000 men, 382 tanks and 335 assault guns to the offensive, backed up by 55,000 men and 561 tanks.[21] To borrow a poker term, the Germans were "all in" to win or lose the war.

One of the worst winters in the region's history made matters even worse for all involved in the Battle. Papa was issued a white winter parka that not only kept him warm but also provided much-needed camouflage. Many soldiers were not as fortunate and had to cover themselves with white sheets to hide their presence.

A special life-saving parka

Bringing down those buzz bombs

Remnants of a buzz bomb

To counter several major German offensives, Papa's unit was relocated a few times to fend off attacks coming from different directions. Papa related that at times he was spread between forty 90mm guns, giving them coordinates upon which to fire. Papa was constantly moved, spending time to the south, northeast and east of Antwerp. How successful was the defense of Antwerp from the buzz bombs? An entire division of anti-aircraft weapons allowed only 211 buzz bombs to land in the critical area of Antwerp.[22] There is no way to know just how many Papa and his unit prevented from arriving at their targeted destination. Ultimately, Antwerp was defended and kept open, the German offensive was defeated and from that point, for all intents and purposes, the war was over. Papa could go home.

Knowing all that did happen, think of how much more would have happened had there been no defenses like Papa helped to provide. There would have been no port, no Antwerp – and victory in Germany would have been delayed, if ever gained at all. You can now understand the importance of the victory at Antwerp.

The Belgian Army "Order of the Day" is a book of honor published by the Belgian government and designates military units recognized for acts of bravery and military virtue. Papa's unit, the 405th AAA Gun Battalion, along with many other units that protected Antwerp, is noted twice in the book. Per a decree of June 17, 1946, number 2509, those units of distinction were granted the right to wear the Belgian Croix de Guerre ribbon and the Fourragère, a shoulder cord worn over the left shoulder of the Army dress uniform.

Papa and his unit finally left Belgium on May 16, 1945 for Cherbourg, France and arrived in Le Havre, France on November 6, 1945 to board the S.S. Mexico Victory. Papa was finally going home along with approximately 2,000 happy but weary soldiers. The "Victory" ships were a cargo ship built to replace ships lost to German submarine attacks. It was designed to be faster and have more range than previously designed ships.

Papa arrived in New York on November 13, 1945 and was sent to Camp Kilmer in New Jersey. Camp Kilmer became the largest processing location for American soldiers heading overseas and returning from World War II. It processed 2.5 million soldiers between 1942 and 1946.[23] Two days later Papa was sent to Fort Indiantown Gap in South Central Pennsylvania, where he was formally discharged on November 18, 1945.

Papa somehow was able to bring home a World War

II German MP 40 Burp Gun with a 9x19mm parabellum cartridge.[24] This was a submachine gun developed by the Germans in 1939. This open-bolt weapon could fire up to 500 rounds per minute. It was often issued to German paratroopers and platoon and squad leaders. He also had a German Walther P38, considered by many to be the best handgun of the war. Papa also retained his own original issue M-1 carbine rifle. No one in the family discussed with Papa where or how he got each of the German weapons. He also had at one time a German helmet and bayonet. He felt guilty about keeping his carbine rifle, however, and would turn it in to the U.S. Government in 1957. He gave away or sold the German weapons as best the family remembers. The family today has many of Papa's World War II artifacts like his dog tags, uniform, duffle bag and mess kits, but it sure would be special to still have those German weapons and helmet. That said, they might have kept a memory alive that Papa did not need.

Praise the Lord! Papa was home at last. Still unsaved and having no knowledge of the Lord Jesus Christ, Papa set out to assimilate back into normal civilian life. It would not be easy but God's plan was still moving forward. Papa was still not aware of that plan but he did know one thing: He was glad to be back in the United States of America.

His son, Rocky, would always relate that Papa, when asked about the War, would only cry and respond, "War is hell!" Papa had experienced 1,367 days in the U. S. Army during World War II. His children would often be terrified as they heard their father's tortured screams during a nightmare, proving the truth of their father's summary – war is indeed hell.

As we close this chapter, allow me to be a bit philosophical. As I reflect on Papa's and my own experiences, I have asked myself from time to time, "Is war morally wrong? Should Christians serve in the military?" I lived for many years in a conservative Mennonite and Amish-dominated region of Pennsylvania. Many there felt strongly that they could not serve in the military. Some became conscientious objectors in order to fulfill their military obligation to the United States.

The Ten Commandments state specifically in Exodus 20:13, "Thou shalt not kill." Some translations of this verse use the word "murder" in place of "kill." Murder is the premeditated killing of another. Many of my high school friends struggled with this decision regarding the military. While World War II saw men and women eagerly enlisting to serve, the Vietnam War brought numerous protests and resistance to the war. The circumstances in that war were very different from World War II. We were attacked on our homeland bringing us into the war. Many deemed our involvement in Southeast Asia as wrong because no such attack ever occurred. The climate of the 1940s was also very different from the 1960s.

I personally felt that serving my country was important and it did not violate my religious beliefs. Of course, I was young, not as strong in my faith as I am now and I was subject to the draft lottery. (If I did not enlist, I would have been drafted.) A pastor named Betty Miller wrote, "God hates war, however, it is necessary to maintain order in the earth and overcome those who would like to destroy good. In fact, the first war ever recorded was the war in heaven where Satan and his evil angels fought against God and his angels. We know this was won by God through Jesus Christ."[25]

The Bible warns us of the increase in wars as the time for Christ's Second Coming approaches. Matthew 24:6-8 states:

> "And ye shall hear of wars and rumours of wars: see that ye be not troubled, for all these things must come to pass, but the end is not yet. For nation shall rise against nation, and kingdom against kingdom: and there shall be famines, and pestilences, and earthquakes, in divers places. All these are the beginning of sorrows."

The Bible speaks many times to war. It often praises the exploits of soldiers against enemies in legitimate battles. War is never a good thing, but sometimes a necessary thing. In a world full of sinful people it is inevitable. 1 Samuel 15:18 says, "And the Lord sent thee on a journey, and said, 'Go and utterly destroy the sinners the Amalekites, and fight against them until they be consumed.'" War is a result of sin. We read in Ecclesiastes 3:8, "A time to love, and a time to hate; a time of war, and a time of peace." Lucifer tried to become like God and led other angels astray, causing their fall from heaven (as explained in the book of Isaiah) and the Book of Revelation depicts the second coming of Christ to be violent. As Papa said, "War is hell," and hell is reality.

I remember a time in 2011 when Papa's family took him to visit an LST (those vehicles that delivered our troops to the beaches) that came to Pittsburgh. It was a proud moment for the family as Papa, in a wheelchair pushed by his grandson Ian, was allowed to pass to the front of the line where it was announced "Soldier Aboard" and all saluted him. It was a remarkable moment as his children, grandchildren and great grandchildren experienced the honor due this great American. I cried as I witnessed him get the respect he so richly deserved!

As he sat in his wheelchair inside the ship, I could only imagine what was going through Papa's mind. The last time he was on such a ship, his life was full of fear and uncertainty. He witnessed death, wondering if he would ever get home safely, surviving devastating conditions. Yet there he was, safe in the arms of his family and God. Yet when Papa came home after the war, it was anything but smooth going. He was about to face one crisis after another, but each one brought him closer to his eventual encounter with Jesus that would change his life and the lives of his family forever. Let's take a closer look at those years after the war in this next chapter.

Part 2

After The Lord

Chapter 6
Coming to the Lord

Upon being discharged from the Army, Papa was a broken man, both physically and mentally. He lived with his father in West Sunbury, Pennsylvania, about twenty miles from Butler, PA. Only the men and woman who experienced the war can explain what it was really like when they came home – and they were hesitant to talk for fear of aggravating their suffering. Papa was alone and jobless. What's more, he came home to find his wife in a relationship with his former best friend and was pregnant to that man. At that point, he had no faith, family or friends to fall back on and he had not yet experienced the grace and love of the Lord. Papa had a couple of odd jobs but nothing significant was available right after the war. Finally, he was offered an opportunity to work at Armco, located in Butler, PA, in late 1945. Armco's main products were carbon, stainless and electrical steel; they were a major employer in the region.

On September 27, 1947, almost two years after his discharge, Papa married Ethel L. Brandon of Emlenton, Pennsylvania, whom he met at a local dance. She was five years younger than Papa and they made a wonderful couple.

They would have three children together: a son, Rockwell and two daughters, Vicki and Denise. Before I tell you more about the family, however, let's take a closer look at the life-changing moment that was at hand for Papa – although he didn't know it.

In those days, workers were not screened and medical history evaluated to determine if they were properly equipped for a job like Papa had at Armco. It was not like today when one can be diagnosed with post-traumatic stress syndrome and other related combat illnesses, which today would have made Papa eligible for assistance from the Veteran's Administration. Jobs at places like Armco were the best jobs available after the war and Papa was pleased to get such an opportunity to provide for his wife and future family. The constant daily pounding of steel presses at the plant, however, ultimately took its toll on Papa. The noise was similar to what Papa had experienced for years during battles in World War II and he eventually lost his mind – literally. On many occasions he would run out of the plant thinking he was still in Germany, and he did it so often that it cost him his job. At home he would go to the refrigerator, take every item out, pile it all on the table and rearrange everything back into the refrigerator, just to occupy his mind. Then he would go to the clothes dresser in the bedroom, take every item out, unfold them, then refold them and put them back again.

After going to the doctor with his wife, Papa was institutionalized at the Butler Veteran's Hospital in November, 1948 with a prognosis of anxiety and neurosis from World War II. During interviews with physicians at the VA Hospital, Papa would break down in tears and start shaking. It was determined he had spent a great deal of time and energy trying to keep his feelings and experiences to himself. I know Papa's son Rockwell was often frustrated because Papa would not get some of these terrible memories off his chest and thus, his mental state was often not healthy.

Like thousands of other soldiers returning home after World War II, Papa got virtually no assistance from the Army or the Veteran's Administration for his problems. This was because they did not know how to address it and because Papa would not talk about it. He never would talk until it became such a burden that he was admitted to the hospital and put in an isolation ward, all alone. In reality, however, he was not alone.

Papa had shown little progress while hospitalized and was given Valium and other depression medications for anxiety. He would tell the doctors that he had participated in four different terrible battles. He was shooting down V-1 and V-2 buzz bombs and then ran for cover as the missile-like devices loaded with bombs would fall around him as well as the other men in his unit. He told them that he had seen thousands of dead soldiers, German and American. One diagnosis was Neurodermatitis, which produced skin lesions caused by anxiety and led Papa to fear he had cancer. Papa was also treated with psychotherapy and the VA even considered shock treatments. All of this made Papa angry, anxious and destructive. Even in his later years during VA examinations, he would still cry when telling the physicians about the war and the killing of other human beings, which conflicted with his eventual strong spiritual beliefs. There was little sign of hope for improvement in Papa's health or mental state in that room in 1948.

Papa and his family would bear the brunt of the effects of stress and anxiety because of this illness. He was in lockdown at the VA hospital in Ward 25, bored and alone. It was almost like solitary confinement. The Bible talks about hell as being a place of torment, loneliness, lack of friendship, and agony, where one is alone with one's thoughts with no rest, day or night. Papa must have been experiencing much of this. Of course, Papa was not in hell because hell will be a place where inhabitants are cut off from God. Little did Papa know that he was not alone. In the solitude of that room, there was Papa, a Gideon's Bible and the presence of God.

Can we possibly comprehend this scenario? What was he thinking about in such a situation? The war? His childhood? His family? The mind is a terrible thing to lose and Papa was not well while left to ponder the past and his future. After several days and nights, for some reason, Papa opened the drawer in a small dresser in his room around midnight. There he found that Gideon's Bible. He knew what it was but had no knowledge of the Gideon's Society or what they did or stood for. Papa had never been exposed to the word of God but he thought he would read some of the Bible anyway, starting at no particular place. He was quickly consumed by its compelling stories and words. After about an hour of reading, he stopped at Matthew

18:3: "Except ye be converted, and become as little children, ye shall not enter into the Kingdom of Heaven." That verse bothered him. He was by then a baptized church member and a regular church attendee but he could not remember being converted.

He knew that converting meant changing from one thing to someone else so he kept reading for three straight hours and kept going back to Matthew18:3. Finally, at about 3:00 am, Papa told me that God spoke to him. Papa said he did not see God but that God had spoken to him in a tangible way and told him that he was going to get out of the hospital. Papa knew he was still behind bars and that the doctors had indicated he was not going to be released any time soon.

During the night, a male nurse came with a flashlight, checking on the patients. The voice of God had been so real that Papa asked the nurse to release him from the restraints that were to keep Papa from escaping. The nurse said he was not to release Papa, but then opened the bars and did release him. Papa walked out of the building to where there was a large oak tree and as Papa stood under it, God spoke to him again. "Howard, you have never been converted. You're a lost sinner." Papa recalled thinking that for the first time in his life, he recognized he was a hell-bound sinner. He dropped to his knees and surrendered his life to Jesus Christ and confessed his sins. He then stood up, looked at the heavens, and said, "Lord, thank you for what you have done and if you heal my affliction and I can get out of this hospital, I'll live for you the rest of my life."

This experience makes one think of Jeremiah 33:3: "Call to me and I will answer you and tell you great and unsearchable things you do not know." I recently read where Michael Youssef of *Leading the Way*, wrote in his monthly journal, "As we seek Him for His will, we learn who He is and we begin to delight in Him and His Will rather than our own. As He becomes the desire of our hearts, we are aligned and ready to receive His Will and vision for our lives."[26]

That was true for Papa. From that point in his life, he would seek the Lord and God's will for his life. Papa went back into the hospital as he had promised to do. Eventually several doctors reexamined him, performed several more tests and then told him, "Mr. Dillaman, we don't know what happened to you, but you're as well as we are. You might as well go home." God had made good on His end of the deal; Papa would make good on his promise to God for the rest of his life.

On November 19, 1948, Papa was deemed well enough to leave, just like that! There was no warning or family notification. Startled and anxious, Papa walked out of the facility and when he got home, his wife thought he was such as new man that they should go to the preacher and get married again. "You're not the same man I married," she would say. Papa had humbled himself before God. In the Old Testament there is an account of when God appeared to Solomon in 2 Chronicles 7:14 and said, "If my people, who are called by my name, will humble themselves and pray and seek my face, and turn from their wicked ways; then will I hear from heaven and will forgive their sin and will heal their land." That is exactly what happened to Papa. He called on the Lord and God healed and released him.

Papa went home and took all of the magazines off the coffee table and put a Bible there instead. He would read through it every year for the rest of his life. He commented to me once that he found "new things" every time he read it. If Papa were alive, I know he would want me to explain to you what happened to him outside that hospital after reading the Gideon's Bible. You may have heard people say, "I came to the Lord," "I gave my life to the Lord," "I got saved," or "I found Jesus." In reality, the Lord found them, just like He did Papa, and offered to exchange their old life for a new life in Christ.

Rock, Howard's son, once stated in a Sunday sermon, "God will not give up on us – even if we've given up on ourselves. He goes out of His way to bring permanent joy to the aching heart." God never gave up on Papa. He will never give up on anyone, including you. Second Peter 3:15 states that the long-suffering of the Lord is for your salvation. He is giving you every opportunity to accept His invitation of salvation. Believing in Christ may happen in a moment, but salvation requires a lifetime relationship with the Lord, being His disciple and responding to His grace and truth as you experience and learn it. The Lord will not wait forever though. Judgment day is one day closer for you (and I) today than it was yesterday.

In every life, there are times of desperation and you may be experiencing one of those times as you read this book. Papa's life is proof that knowing the love and grace of

Jesus Christ takes that desperation and fear away because of what Jesus Christ did on the cross for each and every one of us, including you. Jesus Christ died on a cross and His resurrection gives you the confidence that you will one day overcome death and spend eternity in heaven with Him. John 11:25 says, "I am the resurrection, and the life: he that believeth in me, though he was dead, yet shall he live." Do you believe in the cross and the resurrection? Many have said that the resurrection could not have happened and some try to present evidence to refute it. Whenever I hear this so-called evidence, I think of the story I read in the *Guinness Book of World Records* of the most successful attorney who ever lived, Sir Lionel Luckhoo.

According to the January 1, 1985 edition of the *War Cry* of the Salvation Army, Luckhoo won 245 consecutive murder trial acquittals. He prevailed because of his expert skills to spot flaws in a prosecutor's case and to clearly understand the nature of reliable, admissible and persuasive evidence. He took his expertise in law and applied it to the question of whether or not the resurrection of Jesus Christ stood up to the test of legal evidence. What was Luckhoo's conclusion? "I say unequivocally that the evidence for the resurrection of Jesus Christ is so overwhelming it compels acceptance by proof which leaves absolutely no room for doubt."[27]

Sir Luckhoo then reportedly decided to do the most logical thing in the world after investigating the evidence thoroughly – He gave his life to Jesus Christ. Papa believed in Jesus Christ as his Savior – the Virgin Birth, His dying on the cross and His resurrection! Sir Luckhoo did as well, and so have countless millions through the ages. I urge you to do the same as Papa did if you have not done so already – put your faith in Christ as the One who died for your sins.

Once Papa had put his faith in Christ, he was still facing a major task of rebuilding his life, both inside and out. From that time in the hospital however, until he died, Papa saw Christ do an amazing work that enabled him to live an improbable life, to go from an insanity ward to business, from isolation and loneliness, to family and ministry success. Let's not stop here at the hospital or his going home though, but move on to read more inspiring stories that made up the life of this humble man.

Chapter 7
Life as a Changed Man

When he returned home from the VA hospital, Papa had a new lease on life but needed to find new employment. With his Savior now at his side, he started looking but had no success, so he returned to the steel mill. Papa and Ethel were poor, living in a one-bedroom apartment with a bathroom and kitchen. They owned a floor rug that was in front of their bed and it had become quite soiled. Ethel contacted a vacuum cleaner company to purchase one and soon a door-to-door salesman was at the apartment to give her a demonstration. Both Ethel and Papa were so impressed with the product that they purchased the cleaner. That night, Papa was unable to sleep. God kept him awake, telling him that he wanted him to sell vacuum cleaners door-to-door.

Perhaps you are old enough to remember those door-to-door salesmen representing such companies as Fuller Brush, Charles Chips, various encyclopedias, the milkman and others. Even the television repairman with a truck full of large bulbs made house calls and your family doctor made house calls as well!

This idea for a new job did not sit well with Ethel.

Upon learning of this job, her first words were, "We are going to starve to death!" She said he was crazy and should go back to the hospital. The family always laughs about this story when they hear it now because, while she obviously thought it was true that Papa had experienced a relapse, nothing could have been further from the truth. Papa went about selling Electrolux vacuum cleaners as God had instructed him like there was no tomorrow, door-to-door, day after day. Now if this sounds like an easy task, consider that when Papa started selling the product, it sold for $39.95. The buyer would put $5.00 down and pay $5.00 a month. Papa would fill his vehicle each Monday morning with all of the vacuum cleaners it would hold and hit the road. There were about fifty salesmen assigned to the New Castle, Pennsylvania office and being new, Papa's sales (about two a week) were the lowest. Once all units were sold, it was back to New Castle, Pennsylvania (about 40 miles away) to refill his vehicle with more vacuum cleaners and off he went again. He soon developed an office in his home to repair the cleaners and sell extra bags, hoses and accessories. While Papa sold the product, it was Ethel who ran the office.

One day Papa was cashing his paycheck at a local bank and God again spoke very clearly to him, "Howard, you rob me. I want 10% of what you make." At that time, Papa was putting one dollar in the offering envelope weekly at church and he thought he was generous at that. Papa immediately started giving God ten percent of his income. Can you guess what happened? His sales immediately jumped from two to ten vacuum cleaners a week and he soon led the entire New Castle office in sales. We will discuss more of Papa's value of giving in a later chapter.

God's hand was on Papa. He was not only selling vacuum cleaners, he was spreading the good news of Jesus Christ. Some slammed the door to his message, but Papa was not discouraged. Many bought vacuum cleaners and also learned of a Savior who would change their lives. When Papa made a promise to God, it was his bond. He had promised his Savior he would tirelessly proclaim His name. He might at times have gotten discouraged when looking at his vacuum cleaner sales but he was never discouraged telling others about Jesus.

Actually, he was not discouraged by his sales for long. Papa could sell termites to a lumberyard. Eventually he was one of the top Electrolux salespersons in the Pennsylvania region and America, winning convention trips all over the world. One needed $50,000.00 in annual sales to be allowed to attend the conventions. Papa soon was selling $150,000 worth of vacuum cleaners a year. He won his first sales award in October 1952. My wife Victoria tells me that her mother grew tired of going so often to Boca Raton and other resort locations for Electrolux award ceremonies. They were also regularly going to Hawaii, Ireland, Bermuda, Greece and other exotic places. Papa had a gift of selling and, more importantly, God was using this little man (in stature) to reach thousands as he proclaimed his Savior to those who did not know the Lord.

The Company had a special promotion in 1977-78

whereby the winner would receive a $70,000 home anywhere in the continental U.S. The winner could also take the prize in cash or savings bonds. Keep in mind that $70,000.00 was a lot of money, even today, let alone in 1978. It would be equal to $287,700 in 2013 terms. This kind of money could change one's life dramatically.

All of the Electrolux salespersons hoped they would win the drawing and each received an entry ticket each time they sold a vacuum cleaner. The more they sold, the more entries they had. Several weeks before the drawing, Papa had a premonition from God that he was going to win the drawing Papa trusted in God so much that he announced to all that would listen that he was going to win the prize. Naturally, everyone said, "Sure, Mr. Dillaman, of course you are." They all had been selling as many units as possible and they knew that, while Papa was a top salesman, they too had an excellent opportunity to win this large prize.

Several weeks went by and the day came for the drawing at the national sales banquet, this time in Raleigh, North Carolina. Papa continued to make it clear to all that would listen that "God had selected him to win the drawing." As the president of the company walked to the podium, there was an air of anticipation by all of the salespeople. He reached into the container with thousands of entries, looked at the winner's name, smiled and announced, "The winner of the $70,000 sales award goes to Howard C. Dillaman." That may have been a surprise to many, but not to Papa. After all, he had been telling all who would listen that God had told him weeks ago he would win.

Papa was not at that particular convention but the president of the company called Papa that evening to let him know what happened. Papa told us the conversation went as follows:

President: "Howard, tell me the best news you ever got?"
Papa: "I was saved as Jesus Christ died for my sins!"
President: "No, Howard, what was the next best news you ever got?"
Papa: "That you got saved!"
President: "No, no, no!"
Papa: "I know, I know. I won the $70,000!"

The award landed Papa on the cover of the international trade magazine proclaiming his prize and noted that he had been a member of the vice president's (sales) club every year since 1962. And what did Papa do with that large sum of money? He could have saved it or bought a bigger home or many other things. Instead he spent it on his children. After paying the income taxes on it he purchased each of his three children a new automobile.

Papa continued to excel at sales. His photo regularly appeared in the Electrolux trade magazine extolling his accomplishments. He was nationally recognized for his superior efforts and would enjoy many fruits of success. He always drove a new automobile, usually a Chevrolet, getting a new one almost every year. He wore beautiful suits and dressed his family in the best clothing available, except for Ethel, who was not interested in such things.

VOLUME XLVIII NUMBER 3
MARCH 1978
PUBLISHED BY ELECTROLUX

Best Job Opportunity

ELECTROLUX

NEWS

WINNING BIG

Winner of the $70,000 Payoff is Howard C. Dillman of the New Castle, Pa., Branch. His $70,000 prize is a house built anywhere in the continental U.S.A. or cash or Savings Bonds. Howard has been with Electrolux for 29 years and has been a member of the Vice President's Club every year since 1962.

Newcomer Jim W. Hunter, Anaheim, Calif., Branch, receives the keys to his 1978 Cadillac Coupe de Ville from Southern California Branch Manager Jerry Berman.

The names of these two winners were drawn in March at the Raleigh, N.C., National Sales Cup Banquet.

The magazine cover announcing Papa's big prize

Ethel was always content to wear a housedress and tend to the needs of their three children. She did occasionally like nicer things, but ordinarily it just was not her style. She was beautifully dressed when traveling on the trips they won or excursions to the store but she was just as content to be home caring for the children. Each Saturday, Ethel would go to the hairdresser and shop in downtown Butler. Papa would drive her or she would walk the four or five blocks, as she never learned to drive. Papa discouraged it. Then she would splurge by stopping at the local G.C.

Murphy five and dime store to enjoy lunch and a piece of Boston Cream Pie. Other than church activities, this was pretty much the extent of her travel out of the home.

The *Pittsburgh Post-Gazette* learned of Papa's story and published a nice article about his life and conversion. Papa's story was compelling and he had been speaking for the Lord since he was born again. Conventions, churches, retreats, Rotary Clubs – big and small – they all wanted Papa and he was more than willing to make an appearance.

The family is fortunate to still have many of the notes Papa used in his presentations. He kept hundreds of note cards detailing where and what he had spoken about, complete with Bible passages, conversion stories and sermon highlights. He stuck to the Bible, generally did not interject his personal opinions but often used real life examples. His God is the one and only true God and Papa left you with no doubt as to where he stood.

It was not uncommon for Papa to accept six to eight lay-ministry speaking engagements in a month and sometimes more. I found that he spoke at least 230 times from 1972 through 1995 in places like Ohio (Akron, Warren, Sandusky), West Virginia (Morgantown, Beckley), New York (Corning, Binghamton) and of course Pennsylvania (Philadelphia, State College, Erie).

In the greater Pittsburgh region, Papa was speaking constantly. Consider the large radius he was covering. Often as they got older, one of the children would go along with Papa for an evening or even an overnight trip to a place like an Amish farm in Lancaster County, Pennsylvania.

Rock would go and share his testimony along with Papa's presentation. Papa was a powerful witness – not only for his God but also to his children.

The word was out – Howard C. Dillaman was a speaker who could inspire others for the Lord, sometimes over the protests of his wife. She was responsible to raise three children, manage a home and also manage a vacuum cleaner repair shop and business office. She would tell him she needed him to be home more. Ethel was a believer and supported Papa in his ministry but understood the benefit of balancing the ministry with raising a family. Sometimes Papa was not as thoughtful as she was. He felt a strong calling and could, at times, have a one-track mind. Once Ethel even said to him, "I will be a Christian not because of you but in spite of you." Papa just smiled because he loved Ethel and he knew she loved him.

Of course, Papa did not totally ignore his responsibilities at home. He always made breakfast for the children except on Mondays when he had to be in nearby New Castle early to report to the regional office. He would make fish fillets, sometimes eggs and that nasty carrot juice with celery. Victoria recalls really enjoying those Monday morning breakfasts because her mother would allow the children to have Apple Jacks and Tang. It was a nice break from the fish and juice. When I once mentioned to my wife about a typical breakfast I had growing up, she quickly responded, "No one had it worse than we did because we were stuck with fish **every day.**" I had to laugh even though she did not find it very funny. Papa was always home for dinner, although he often went back out in the evening, either for a sales call or a ministry speaking engagement. One of Papa's popular themes when speaking was reciting a message he had found and tweaked it to his life. It was typed and glued as an insert in his Bible. I love reading it and think you will, too:

> Seventeen years ago, about the time I came to Electrolux Company, I was introduced to a man and since then this man has become my greatest and dearest friend, and due to His position in life, He has been able to help me with every endeavor I have undertaken without exception.
>
> This man I am speaking of was born in an obscure village, the child of a peasant woman. He grew up in another obscure village and worked in a carpenter's shop until He was 30 years of age. Then for three years he was an itinerant preacher. He never wrote a book. He never went to college. He never held an office. He never owned a home. He never had a family. He never did one of the things that usually accompany greatness. He had no credentials but Himself.
>
> While still a young man, the tide of popular opinion turned against Him. He was turned over to His enemies. His closest friends deserted Him. He went through the mockery of a trial. He was nailed to a cross between two thieves. While dying, His executioners gambled for the only piece of property He owned, and that was his coat. When He died, He was taken down and laid in a borrowed grave through the pity of a friend.
>
> Nineteen centuries have come and gone, and today

He is the centerpiece of the human race and the leader of the column of progress.

I am not far within the mark when I say that of all the armies that ever marched, all the navies that ever sailed, all the parliaments that ever sat, and all of the kings that ever reigned, put together, have not affected the life of man upon this earth as powerfully as this one solitary life. I present to you my friend, my manager, and my counselor, Jesus Christ, not for debate but for decision.[28]

This is a remarkable piece of work, simple but profound. I can almost hear Papa reciting this in a firm, powerful voice. Papa was an incredible man because he allowed God to prepare him and then he acted upon that preparation. Someone once defined luck as when preparation meets opportunity. Papa did not lead folks to the Lord by luck or chance. He did it by taking advantage of his God-given gifts. Papa simply loved Jesus Christ – there is no other way to say it!

Are you "born again" or just a religious unconverted person? Those who believe in Christ are dead to sin but alive to God (Romans 6:11). What an example Papa was. No matter where he was or what he was doing, he first was alive in the Lord. He understood Philippians 2:13: "For it is God who works in you to will and to act according to His good purpose." God will never ask you to do anything without giving you the provision to do it and do it well. The Holy Spirit was working through Papa. As Jesus told the apostles in Acts 1:8, "You will receive power, after that the Holy Spirit is come upon you; and ye shall be witnesses unto me both in Jerusalem, and in all Judea, and in Samaria, and unto the uttermost part of the earth." I certainly saw that truth operating in Papa's life.

But now, let's find out a little bit more about what it was like living and growing up with this man mightily used by the Lord. As I stated earlier, Papa was not a perfect man (who is?) and his family saw him at his best and at his worst. In my mind, that only makes how God used him in even more improbable and inspiring ways. At times, we may think that someone who serves the Lord is perfect or above the problems of life. Yet Papa knew that he was an imperfect man and only the return of the Lord would change him completely into the person that Jesus wanted him to be. Papa successfully raised a wonderful family, of which I am the beneficiary, and their stories will make you laugh and cry. Let's go there together to read some of those stories now.

Chapter 8
Howard's Wife and Children

As I mentioned earlier, in 1947 a justice of the peace married Papa and Ethel. Howard remembered Ethel as a beautiful woman who was easy-going and fun to be around. She was destined to be a great wife, mother, cook and alto in the church choir. Their first home was on Ridge Avenue in Butler, Pennsylvania. Papa was then working at Armco and Ethel was a homemaker.

Papa and Ethel

It was not long before their first child, Rockwell, came into the world on April 8, 1949. He was (and is) a redhead and redheads were common throughout the extended family. Rockwell was all boy, interested in playing sports in the neighborhood and in music. He would excel in the classroom when he applied himself but his special gift at the time was in music. I say "at the time" because Rock, or Rocky as we call him in the family, found an even greater gift later in life. While all of the children would be exposed to music, Rockwell was the one to develop a love that he has maintained throughout his life. Starting on the piano, he would later add the trumpet. He even directed the music for *Guys and Dolls* for his high school senior play. Like most men, Papa was proud to have a son. He wanted Rock to be a pastor, but Rock was more interested in music. Rock eventually married and has three children and also five grandchildren.

Victoria Lynn was born in December 1954, giving Papa his first daughter over whom he could dote. He even named his boat the "Vicki Lynn." Victoria also played the piano and clarinet. She was involved in the high school band, the Sequinettes, a Rockette-type performance group and the Usher's Club, a team that ushered at numerous high school events, such as stage productions, graduation and other performances. She eventually took a serious liking to tennis, in which she excelled. Later in life, she added interior decorating as a hobby, at which I think she could have made a living if she so desired. She still loves panning through magazines and websites for decorating ideas and tips. Many ask her advice when planning a new home or renovation. She would have two sons and a daughter and three grandchildren to enjoy.

Rock and Karen Dillaman

My bride and I

The final child, Denise Lee, was born in 1956. Denise also played the piano and clarinet, but showed little interest in any particular extracurricular activity. She would find her calling as an aerobics instructor and professional painter along with being a wife and mother of two sons. She was, per Papa, probably the biggest challenge of all of the three

Denise with her husband Joe

children when she was growing up. She was always the one who seemed to test her parents' patience.

Refusing to go to school unless driven, scuffing the toes of new shoes or refusing to be quiet when put to bed were just some of the antics for which she became known. Yes, we all did things like that, but Papa reported that she seemed to take that behavior to another level. Rock and Victoria both spoke of how Denise would pester everyone until they would strike back and then she would run crying to Papa. Of course, Papa did not investigate – he just got out his belt. Remember, Papa did not like confrontation. In spite of all their challenges and childish ways, Papa loved and was proud of his two daughters and son. Papa wanted his children to appreciate music, education and extracurricular activities. I suspect this was because he never had such an opportunity himself. He wanted them to enjoy the fruits of his success and experience life as he had not been able to.

Victoria has often told me what a dapper dresser Papa was, immaculate from head to toe. She would say,

"How did a man that grew up with nothing know so much about style?" They resided in a simple home on a busy street with a gasoline station across the road. That made for a busy neighborhood. Victoria loved lying at the end of her bed at night, listening to the sounds of the city – conversations on the sidewalk, squealing tires, motorcycles, thunderstorms, birds – listening and watching it all was part of growing up.

The children were raised in a strict environment that Papa established and enforced. The children often turned to their mother for relief from Papa who could become angry. This anger and anxiousness was a carryover from his war illness. If he had a stressful day or was not feeling well, all knew to be quiet and leave Papa alone. He would pace the hallways and be stressed. Rock recalls times when, during the night, as the family was asleep, he could hear Papa, in bed, yelling, "Jesus! Jesus! Jesus!" He felt bad and knew that his father was being tormented by something. Over the years, Rock encouraged Papa to talk out his anxiety, but Papa just kept it inside. Ethel was the peacemaker and allowed the children some latitude to relax and play – and be children.

Bible teaching was a daily family activity every evening after all had their baths and were ready for bed. Papa was a serious man and expected the children to take their schoolwork and Bible studies seriously. When the children watched a television show, Papa would often express his thoughts that it was a waste of time – but he did not stop them from watching. Ethel was more accommodating to allow the children to have some fun. My wife Victoria often says, "We were never allowed to have fun as children. No movies, no dances, no cards, no board games, no fun." How ironic that Papa met his wife at a dance but did not want his children to attend dances! One of the times Victoria enjoyed the most was when Papa would go to the driving range in the evening to hit a bucket or two of golf balls. The family came along, sitting in the car with the children in their pajamas, enjoying an ice cream cone.

Papa was strict about many things and the rules also applied to his wife. Recently I was looking through the television listing of what was on that evening and I came across *Dr. Zhivago*. I asked Victoria, "Did you ever see the movie *Dr. Zhivago*?" She related she had and would never forget going to see that movie. I knew the 1965 film starring Omar Sharif and Julie Christie was famous but I was surprised she thought so much of it, especially because she was only 11 years old at the time. She explained that her mother wanted to see the movie but could not go because she knew Papa would be upset. Victoria was instructed by her mother to lie if asked and tell Papa they were going to the doctor. So off they went to the Penn Theater in Butler. Papa never found out they went to the movie that day but Victoria will never forget being scared that Papa would learn of the trip to the movies and that she had lied. Papa had put that kind of fear even into his wife.

The same was true with Ethel learning how to drive. She wanted to learn but Papa was her teacher so there was no chance of her learning. He would have her in tears before the session was over and she gave up. Deep down,

Papa wanted her at home and he was going to ensure she could not drive. Ethel was happy when Victoria got her driver's license. That allowed Victoria, her mother and sister to go about 20 miles away to the Murrysville Mall for the day. The three girls could shop, eat dinner out and have fun together. They even brought home an egg custard pie each time for Papa.

When Papa told his kids to be quiet, he meant it. If they were not, they were going to have an encounter with his belt. Rocky told me that Papa had the fastest belt in the land. He could not believe how fast Papa could get his belt off of his waist. Victoria remembers an incident when Denise was about fourteen years old. Denise was hanging out with some of her friends at a local burger hut when Papa showed up angry about something. He spanked her with his belt right in front of her friends and in public.

Victoria once had forgotten to wash the kitchen floor on another occasion and instead went out with her friends. Upon returning home, Papa again used his belt, much to the astonishment of one of Victoria's girlfriends who came home with her. Victoria was clear that Papa did not abuse or beat the children but he did hit them hard enough to get their attention. It is currently trendy not to spank or discipline one's children. Spankings were commonplace years ago. I was spanked with a belt or a tree switch many times. Looking back, I must admit I deserved the punishment – maybe not always, but most of the time. Most likely, Papa was disciplined the same way and it carried over to the way he handled those situations.

It was not uncommon on Sunday afternoons after church and Sunday school for Papa to play the record, *Flight F-I-N-A-L*. My wife Victoria remembers how scared she became when it played and she would hide under the dining room table to keep from hearing it. She was about four years old at the time. The record was released in the 1950s, sold over one million copies and was written and produced by Forrest McCullough.

The beginning of the record starts with interviews in an airport and then you hear the captain, "Your attention please, I am your captain. The flight thou art making today is the same which Abraham, Moses, John, Peter, Paul, and all of those redeemed before have made. Enoch and Elijah joined us in mid-flight, without passing through the Gate of Death. We shall be flying today at altitudes unlimited and at a speed never known to thee before. Flying time to the New Jerusalem is not considered, for thou are now in the realm known as Eternity, where Time is no more. As we left the Earth, the weather was stormy with heavy overcast, but the report from the New Jerusalem is, as it always will be, a beautiful day without a cloud."

McCullough added, "This record is meant to be a dramatic rendition and passengers need merely have their ticket stamped with the blood of Christ. Your seatbelt is Psalm 23. No meals will be served on this flight, as you're about to gorge yourself at the Great Banquet Table upon arrival. So pack your bags and let's jet away from this mortal coil! But don't bother bringing your earthly burdens, as these have recently been banned by the TSA."[29]

Papa was an enthusiastic Christian and at times could almost come across as fanatical. Papa was not ashamed of his faith and never was one to shy away from proclaiming his belief in Jesus Christ. There are times when he went a bit overboard, but keep in mind where he had come from to where he was. He was so grateful to God for his new life that he did not want to do anything to disappoint the Lord or go back on that promise he made in the VA Hospital to give his all for the Lord. We all have been "embarrassed" by things our parents have said or done, particularly while we were teenagers. Can you imagine going on a date with your father driving the car (no one was of age to drive) and the car had a small plate attached to the dashboard that read, "Caution: Driver may suddenly disappear?" Victoria relates that none of her friends knew what the rapture was (it is a Christian belief that the believers will be taken away from earth right before the Second Coming of Jesus) and thought her dad was crazy.

The family's typical Sunday was much like the ones I had when I grew up. No work was to be performed; not any! The family went to worship God, attend Sunday school and then enjoy a day of strict rest. That meant no lawn mowing, no playing in the yard, no nothing. It was the Sabbath and Papa kept it that way. As a child I remember my grandmother cooking the Sunday meal on Saturday night because she did not want to work on Sunday any more than necessary. That was a carryover from her strict Dutch upbringing when she was raised in the Netherlands.

A common annual trip for the family in the '60s and

'70s was a one-week stay at Mahaffey Camp, a Christian campground in Western Pennsylvania. The camp was founded in 1894, with the Alliance Western Pennsylvania District purchasing it in 1919. Thousands over the years would come to teach, preach and hear the gospel on this property. The Lord has surely used that place over the years. The entire family, except Papa, went on Monday morning. Papa would arrive Monday evening after reporting his vacuum sales to the Electrolux home office. Papa had purchased a house trailer for the family to live in during their weekly stay and then left it at the church campground for the balance of the year. Therefore,it needed some serious cleaning before it could be used again each year. Victoria was not too keen on cleaning the trailer but loved the week at the campground that was a week of Christian teaching and fellowship.

Rocky was invited to speak at the camp in 2012 and sure enough, the trailer was still there – in pretty good condition and still being used. Papa had donated the trailer to the Camp. Rock has related that just seeing that trailer again brought back great memories of Christian fun, fellowship and growth. On the way home, the family would stop for dinner. Of course, Papa wanted everyone to order the same food and water. The family members all wanted something different more in line with their personal tastes. Papa would say, "Why can't you just get meatloaf or a hamburger? Why always something different?" It was not long before Ethel solved the dilemma by saying, "Let them get what they want – you old skin flint!"

Papa and Ethel loved their children and grandchildren and they all loved to come to their home. Papa and Ethel were known for having great treats in their basement: Donald Duck orange juice, dried almonds, Little Debbie oatmeal pies and meat sticks – lots of good stuff. Victoria's son Ian first called Howard "Papa" when he was 18 months old and the name stuck from that point forward. Papa had several three-wheeled electric cars that the kids loved to ride. In later years, he had a pool table for all to enjoy. Jason Dillaman, Rock's son, remembers a local neighbor and car dealer storing a 1979 Cadillac Coupe Deville in Papa's garage. It was special – pure white with a red interior. All of the children and grandchildren had lots of great memories from visits to the house. Papa loved all of the grandchildren, but he seemed to particularly love the boys. He bought Victoria's sons nice leather bomber jackets and many other things.

Christmas was typical with a beautiful tree and presents for all. Papa always got Ethel something nice. Papa and Ethel respected the Sabbath and thus, if Christmas fell on a Sunday, the presents could be opened but no toys could be played with until Monday. The biggest difference from most people's Christmas was that once all of the presents had been opened, Papa would come around with an envelope for each child. When they were young the envelope would contain $10 or $20. As they got older, however, $50 or even $100 was the gift. I must say that Santa never appeared like that at my house! Rocky told me that he was aware when he was young that they were better off than most families. Victoria has told me many times that they lacked for nothing they needed. Papa and Ethel had been greatly blessed by the Lord.

After spending the morning together, the family usually traveled a few miles to West Sunbury to spend some time with Papa's father Fred and his family. Thanksgiving was a holiday for staying home and spending time with the immediate family, but Christmas was a time for celebrating with the extended family.

Family was very important to Papa. He knew what it was like to have a limited family, losing his mother at a young age. Once he became a born again Christian, family was even more important to him. He wanted his family to know the Lord, including his extended family. And the thought of having a pastor in the family always thrilled Papa, which again is part of the improbable story of this amazing man. He grew up with no knowledge of God, met the Lord under trying circumstances, lived and served in a rural community outside Pittsburgh, and had no formal education, but was transformed into a giant of a man for the Lord and the things of God. His son Rock did go into ministry and has served in Pittsburgh at one church for 30 years, as of this writing. Thus Howard's influence and inspiration continues through all the children and grandchildren, but had a unique expression through Rock. Let's look at Rock's call and the role that Papa played in his pastor son's life and development.

Chapter 9
One Proud Papa

Rock grew up as a kid loving the times the family spent together, but at times struggling and even rebelling against his father's commitment to church and discipline. While growing up, Rock could get into trouble in the neighborhood just like all kids. Papa was quick to punish when he thought the kids were out of line. Once a neighbor lady left 50 cents on her garbage can along the street to tip the pickup man. The money never made it to the trash man and she accused Rock of stealing it. Rocky proclaimed his innocence but Papa was having no part of it. Papa grounded Rock for his misbehavior. Several days later, the neighbor came to Papa and told him that she had learned that someone else had stolen the money and that Rocky was innocent. Papa actually apologized to Rock and related how proud he was of him. Maybe Papa also learned not to be so quick to judge.

Please don't misunderstand; Rock was no angel. He would regularly push back against his strict upbringing. At times he had enough of the constant nightly Bible study, moral instruction and coaching, feeling that the church was too legalistic. He resented it being forced on him. He was known to cause trouble in Sunday school and while sitting in the balcony during church services with friends, developed a poker game, making cards out of offering envelopes. Once Rock was older it was difficult for Papa to catch him or punish him. After chasing Rock for a short distance, Papa would say, "If I have to, I'll chase you down and it will be worse when I catch you!" That usually caused Rock to give up and take the whooping. This rebellion toward his faith followed Rock through his college years.

By the age of eighteen, Rock wanted no part of his father's God. In fact, Rock has related more than once that he told his father, "Once I leave this house, I will never darken the door of a church again!" To say that to Papa was breaking his heart and Rock knew it. Papa knew, however, that he himself had lived without the Lord for many years and that prayer would help heal Rock's heart. Papa was the first believer in his entire family so this was not the first time Papa had experienced someone refusing the love of Jesus Christ.

Rock went to Duquesne University in Pittsburgh to major in music after graduating from Butler Senior High School. To this day, he is a talented musician. On a break from college, he was home and charged with overseeing his two younger sisters while Papa was away on another company function and his mother was shopping downtown. That evening, the girls found Rock crying in front of the television set. Further inquiries determined that Rocky was watching a Billy Graham Crusade and had accepted Jesus Christ as his Savior.

I spoke to Rock at length about this experience. He related that he had flopped on the couch to watch television and since there were only three channels back then, he just happened to come across a Billy Graham Crusade. He realized upon listening to Dr. Graham that he had strayed from his upbringing and immediately committed his life to the Lord.

When his mother returned home, she could tell he had been crying and asked why. He told her what happened and that he wanted to immediately talk with Papa to tell him the exciting news. Papa was away on a business trip and rarely called home. Rock went to his bedroom and started praying that his father would call home that evening. Soon, his mother answered the ringing telephone and Rock could tell from the conversation that it was his father. His mother informed Papa that Rock had something to share with him, called Rock down from his room and handed him the telephone. Rock shared with Papa what had happened and he could tell how happy Papa was on the telephone. Papa told Rock to get on his knees and Papa prayed for both of them and thanked God for the experience.

Papa would later say that when he returned to his hotel room that evening, he felt that God was telling him something was happening back home and that he should call. That is an amazing story. How did those kinds of things – those spiritual coincidences – keep happening to Papa? I think it is because God was able to use Papa in so many ways because Papa was listening and available. And He wants to do the same with you, if only you will let go and let Him work in your life. The foundation of Rock's faith had been established by his upbringing. This was the means by which God would get Rock back on the path. We can all stray and question what is going on in our life. What is important is that we get back on the path to life and grace.

Rock would soon leave Duquesne University for Nyack College in New York to begin his pastoral studies. He would return home only at holidays and in the summer. Only eleven of his fifty-one credit hours transferred to Nyack, so he was almost starting college all over again. While in high school during church youth activities, Rock had met a young lady, Karen Staley, who would always hang out with the pastor's daughter. Karen had come to know the Lord through this friendship with the pastor's daughter. Karen was a year younger than Rock and after high school coincidentally she also went to Nyack College.

They started dating (Rock asked her out on a dare) and they were engaged a year later. Papa liked Karen and told Rock he should marry her, and even went along with Rock to purchase the engagement ring. They were married by the time Rock graduated in 1973. He then attended Asbury Theological Seminary in Wilmore, Kentucky. Rocky would pastor churches in New Castle (one year) and North East (seven years), both in Pennsylvania, and finally accepted the pastoral responsibilities at Allegheny Center Alliance Church (ACAC), an urban church on the North Side of Pittsburgh, Pennsylvania. In 1984 Papa helped Rock and Karen financially as they progressed through their ministry training. Papa would show up at the church with a brand new automobile to help them out. Rock recalls this happening four or five times, and Papa usually came with a Buick or Mercury Brougham.

ACAC was no typical assignment. Many discouraged Rock from accepting this challenging call. Rock once said, "I am not sure God is doing the right thing in my life!" Papa, with the hair standing up on the back of his neck, red faced and pointing his finger at Rock told him, "Do not *ever* question the character of God!" Rock not only accepted the challenge but also has helped, over the last thirty years, to build one of the strongest churches in the Christian and Missionary Alliance denomination. Pastor Rock was quoted on January 10, 2000, in the *Pittsburgh Post-Gazette* while leading worship services to pray for Pittsburgh community leaders:

> "When I arrived in 1984, there were about 400 members in the church. Today, there are over 4,000 members with an average Sunday attendance of 2,800. We were mostly a white, drive-in congregation. It was a case like a lot of older churches where the community in which the church was located had changed, people had moved out and drove back on Sundays to attend the church. In the ensuing 16 years, we felt that while we're a metropolitan church, we needed to intentionally minister to the North Side (of Pittsburgh) community in which we were located. We also felt we needed to become a racially diverse congregation that represented the larger community. That meant more North Siders and more minorities joining the church. Currently (2000), there are more than 500 African American

members in the congregation. Many congregations talk about becoming more diverse but ACAC had success because the congregation changed in order to be more welcoming. The changes affected the music program as well as the education offered in Sunday School, and minorities soon assumed leadership roles."[30]

In the same *Post-Gazette* article, Pittsburgh Mayor Thomas Murphy commented, "Dillaman's message is how the role of the church is not simply for personal restoration – it is also that to get personal restoration you need to work within your community."[31]

While Papa was always proud of his children (well, most of the time), he was particularly proud of Rock's Christian endeavors. Not only was Rock the oldest child and only son but also Papa was especially proud that Rock was in the ministry. This ministry would impact many aspects of a diverse community and one that is not afraid today to confront innercity issues. It is a model church with emphasis on the slogan, "Following Jesus in diverse community." It strives to constantly worship, grow, serve and share.

As an example, the church recently purchased a nuisance bar, putting it out of business and providing an opportunity for a faith-based business to operate in that location. Papa was proud to hear Rockwell preach and even enjoyed preaching alongside him on several occasions. To have a son in the ministry was something Papa liked to brag about, and rightly so. Thousands have accepted Jesus Christ as their Lord and Savior as a result of Rock's leadership guided by the Holy Spirit. Papa had raised Rock to listen to the Holy Spirit in his ministry and obey. Rock still remembers Papa's instruction, "Go, give and pray!"

My good friend, John Kailer, has expressed to me numerous times how grateful he is to Papa for the Christian influence he had on his son and Rock's dedication to proclaim the gospel. In November 1992, John's parents visited ACAC from their home in Albuquerque, New Mexico, attending a normal Sunday morning worship service with John and his wife, Debbie. After a powerful sermon on John 3 and the need for one to be "born again," Rock led a simple sinner's prayer for those who wanted to make a commitment to faith in Christ that day. Rock asked people in attendance to bow their heads and close their eyes to repeat a prayer after him. He then asked those in attendance to raise their hand to indicate that they had prayed and put their faith in Christ.

Once the service was completed, as the family was leaving the service, John's father, J.D. Kailer, said he wanted a moment to meet Rock. It turned out that he had been one of the ten or so who had raised their hand during the prayer. He had made a commitment to the Lord that day and his wife would also join him within a couple of years. John spoke at his father's memorial service (age 92) in 2014 and shared that after 50 years of attending a church where there was no clear emphasis on Jesus Christ and God's Holy Word, his parents had found and joined a church where their faith was encouraged and strengthened.

When Victoria and I married in 2006, I relocated to

Pittsburgh. We discussed at length what church we would regularly attend. I had attended Rock's church on several occasions while we were dating and really felt the Spirit there. Although it would be a 20-mile drive each way, we committed to Allegheny Center Alliance Church (ACAC). Looking back, I am so grateful that was the direction we went. I grew up in a conservative, Caucasian church and that was the case at all of the other churches I attended as I progressed through life. My upbringing was to sit quietly in the pew with my family, listen and behave. No one ever yelled "Amen" when we were so moved while the pastor preached and certainly no one ever raised his or her hands to heaven in joy during worship.

While my childhood choir and music were good, it quite frankly could not compare to what I now experience at ACAC. There are about eight hundred people worshipping together per service, and I had never attended a church service that had more than a couple of hundred worshippers. I got involved in the deacon ministry to assist members in need and my eyes were really opened. For the first time in my life, I saw and heard the issues with which some inner city residents were involved on a daily basis. The congregation was very generous in funding this ministry and those needs.

Rock has tirelessly served ACAC. Often he would preach all five Saturday and Sunday services. Rock has many skills, but I believe his greatest calling is the pulpit. The church administration soon realized that five live services were too many for all of the pastors so a video system was installed. This allowed the pastors to preach one or two services live and use video for the others. This worked well, but often Rock would override the procedure and preach live. He just felt it was what he was called to do. Well, while it felt right, it created a great deal of stress for him. Add to that life's trials and tribulations and you have a person ripe for a problem if he doesn't take the necessary precautions. Sure enough, in March 2014 Rock had a serious heart attack from which he has made a complete recovery – while making some adjustments to his work lifestyle.

This church that Rock has served so faithfully has helped me grow in my faith. Rock is a committed servant of the Lord with wonderful pulpit gifts. ACAC is a place where Jesus Christ is worshiped and the Bible taught. There is one clear message: Jesus Christ is Lord and Savior. The Bible is the one true word of God. There are no book sales, no prosperity promises and no discarding of crutches in dramatic healing services.

And of course, this great ministry overseen by this wonderful pastor was due in large part to Papa. Papa's improbable life has impacted thousands of people through his son. Who would have ever thought this possible from where Papa had started or the condition he was in after the War? This story should inspire you to be faithful where you are and trust the Lord to use you in great and mighty ways. When you are faithful, God is even more faithful to the promises in His word.

Howard C. Dillaman trusted God and God took that trust and multiplied it through a son who pastors a thriving church. And legacy is important, for none of us are getting out of here alive – all of us will one day pass into the presence of the Lord. It has been said that the true test of a man is not how he lives but how he dies. Papa had passed the living test, but let's now take a look at Howard's last years to see if he finished his faith journey as well as he had started it. I am sure you will find this chapter of Papa's life as inspirational as what you have already read.

Chapter 10
Final Years of Papa's Life

While Papa's life had many special and inspiring moments, it is important to look at his final years to really grasp the impact he had on people's lives. As you know by now, Papa never wasted an opportunity to tell anyone about the Lord. And I so mean *anyone* – large or small, young or old, male or female, rich or poor. Papa proved there is no such thing as being too old to learn, grow and be excited about the Lord. The greatest deeds of Moses were when he was between the ages of 80 and 120. Noah was 500 years old when he built the ark. Abraham was an old man when he fathered Isaac. John Wesley, the Christian theologian credited along with others as the founder of Methodism, was ashamed at age 86 because he could only preach twice a day. (He is said to have preached more than 40,000 sermons in his lifetime.) One does not retire from proclaiming the good news of Jesus Christ as Savior.

This would apply not only to the public at large but also to Papa's family. It wasn't so much that he told you all the time about the Lord, but how he conducted his life. Will Graham, the grandson of the great evangelist Billy Graham, once said, "I knew Dr. Graham as my grandfather while I was young. He was a humble man. Only later in life did I realize the greatness of the Lord." I suspect a similar thing happened with Papa's family. They knew him as a father and grandfather; a great humble man. But as they grew up, they realized what a magnificent thing the Lord had done through him. There was never any doubt that Papa was the Lord's servant and proud to be so.

Papa was determined to take care of himself after the passing of Ethel, his wife of 38 years. She passed away in April 1985 from an unusual disease called Chronic Polymyositis, an idiopathic inflammatory myopathy that causes muscle weakness. Papa had taken care of her as she progressed through the stages of a slow, agonizing death, comforted in knowing that she would soon be with the Lord. She was a dear woman, loved by all. Jason Dillaman, Rock's son, only has memories of his grandmother being in bed. He took great joy in climbing up in bed with her, giving her hugs and kisses. Papa eventually remarried but it was not the best situation. Loneliness can make one do things he or she normally would not do. None of us are perfect and sometimes the choices we make are wrong ones. Papa did not believe in divorce so he lived separately from her for the last years of his life.

Papa was not one to waste money, almost to a fault. As a product of the Great Depression, he was frugal in many aspects of life. He often kept the lights low or off in his home, did not have cable television and saved plastic bags and aluminum foil in case of a special need. He maintained a healthy diet. He was an early riser and headed for bed soon after dark. He ate one half of a banana each morning. No one can remember his weight ever being anything but five pounds on either side of 130. His house was very modest. The flashiest thing I remember about his home was the mounted marlin he had caught on an Electrolux fishing trip during a convention he had attended.

His daily routine started with a three-mile walk at the local mall. There were several other "locals" at the mall each morning but they were more interested in visiting with each other, sharing a cup of coffee. Papa wanted to walk and "praise the Lord" if the opportunity presented itself so he greeted everyone. He kept a brisk pace, making at least five trips around the inside of the mall. Once he spotted someone that he had not seen before, he would approach that individual, tell them that the Lord loved them and offer his booklet, which we will talk about in chapter 12. If the person positively responded, he would pray with them, say "God Bless" and start walking again.

After his walk, he went home to read his Bible and the newspaper, tend to the house, maybe pay some bills, pray and then pray some more. He had a list of prayer concerns that had more than 40 names and all got mentioned in his prayers. Papa was a great believer in prayer. I was once reviewing his prayer list with him and noted that someone on the list has passed away. I told Papa and he said, "You're right but I will keep praying for their families."

He drove until he was 85 years of age, when the family finally became concerned for everyone's health and took away his driving privileges. Papa protested a little, but recognized it was time to give it up. He attended church each week and his daughter Denise usually took him once he needed assistance getting there. He played his harmonica as the special music once every three months at church, providing entertainment to which everyone looked forward. In fact, he played on the Sunday his church celebrated his 90th birthday, providing a stirring rendition of *When The Roll is Called Up Yonder*, written by James M. Black in 1893, and another of his favorites, *Do Lord, Remember Me.*

It was always fun to get the entire family together for a holiday like Thanksgiving or Christmas. After lots of food, we would eventually all gather together and talk about things of the past. Papa always got the biggest, most comfortable chair and he would play his harmonica. He was so good and had several harmonicas he would play, varying in size from about one and one-half inches in length to a standard six inch. He knew so many songs right off the top of his head. It was such a treat and, of course, the grandchildren had rarely heard a harmonica played so they loved it. Years before, Papa played a mandolin but he had given it to a friend so I never had the pleasure of hearing him play it. I am told he was a wonderful player. He would not sing but he sure could play.

Often the family would start talking about their childhoods while the grandchildren were running around and playing. There were lots of laughs and Papa would even tell a joke or story. They were always the same each visit but we laughed anyway, as Papa loved telling them. While Papa was hard on his children, he could not get enough for his grandchildren – new clothes or toys, whatever was needed when they were young. It is now a shame that a couple of years after Papa's death that the entire family no longer gets together due to some internal strife. Papa would not be very happy about that!

It wasn't long before Papa could no longer live alone since we were concerned about a couple of falls he had and if he was taking his medications as scheduled. Papa had often made it clear to the family that a nursing home was not in his future. This is often a difficult situation for many families, since they are concerned about how to handle elderly family members in their later years. As part of God's plan, however, there was still a special part of Papa's life yet to play out, even at his age.

His granddaughter-in-law, Stacey, had previously been an assistant in a local nursing home and felt she could take care of Papa. It was a decision the entire family was comfortable with. This was no small commitment. The needs of an 85-year-old man in addition to being married with three children (ages 9, 6, and 1) could overwhelm anyone. Sometimes it did overwhelm Stacey. But the Lord blessed her family, which was a greater return than any investment she made in Papa's care.

Stacey and her husband Ian were such a loving and attentive couple to Papa. Stacey wanted this challenge and God used Papa to impact her life. Stacey had not been raised in a Christian home and had never been exposed to the Lord in any way. She also had experienced significant tragedy in her life. She was divorced at a young age with two small children and had experienced the loss of her mother and a brother to violent crime while her father provided minimal attention. She married my son-in-law, Ian, in 2006. He brought stability to her life and together they had a beautiful daughter, Sophia, adding to her existing family of sons Austin and Cameron. Although Ian had been raised in the church, they did not attend very often. Of course Papa changed all of that! He still went to church every week and Ian, Stacey and family started going with him.

Ian and Stacey with their children Cameron, Austin and Sophia

Their entire family saw an example of what it was like to be Christ-like. Papa taught them to be thankful at meals for God truly deserved thanks for His provision. He showed them that each day started and ended in prayer – on his knees. He did not allow anyone to take the Lord's name in vain. The change in the household was dramatic and obvious. My wife and I often commented about the change. We all felt that the Lord had put Papa in their midst to be cared for, but also to teach them and be an example. Sophia (the youngest) loved Sunday school.

Stacey was fabulous at tending to Papa and the entire extended family felt blessed that Papa was in a comfortable, safe and loving place. Papa could no longer sell vacuum cleaners or walk the mall to praise the Lord, but he was not done spreading the glorious name of Jesus Christ! He had another special friend in the house and that was Emma, a five-year-old Boston Terrier; who never left his side because free food was always available from Papa. I think Emma gained 8-10 pounds as Papa's sidekick, eating everything from burgers, pizza, vanilla wafers and even soup. Papa just threw it on the floor and Emma disposed of it.

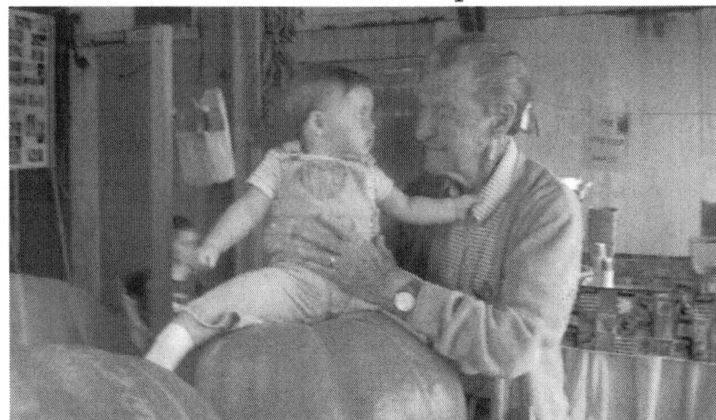

Papa with Sophia when she was 14 months old

As we all advance towards our later years, we wonder what it will be like. Will my family take care of me? Will I be a burden to them? Will I be alone? Well, Papa had the Lord at his side and he shadowed him from testimony to testimony. He brought the light of Jesus Christ into a household, transforming all who were members. Papa even had a huge impact on Stacey's family when they came to her home to visit her. He was a friend to all and a great example for the Lord.

Slowly, Papa's health deteriorated and he was confined to bed. He loved visitors and always flashed that great smile when you entered the room. Papa's sight was now set on heaven. The apostle Paul wrote in Colossians 3:1, "If ye then be risen with Christ, seek those things which are above, where Christ sitteth on the right hand of God." Jonathan Edwards, the great Puritan preacher, spoke of Heaven when he said, "It becomes us to spend this life as a journey toward heaven...to which we should subordinate all other concerns of life. Why should we labor or set our hearts on anything else, but that which is our proper end and true happiness?" D.L. Moody, on his deathbed said, "Earth recedes – Heaven opens before me!" Death is not something most of us like to think or talk about. Yet, it is an inevitable event, for none of us are getting out of here alive! Many spend their time pursuing earthly success but should be preparing themselves for their place in eternity.

Papa had lived a great life filled with incredible contrasts. Born poor, losing his mother at a young age, living through the Depression, serving heroically in World War II, struggling with mental illness from the war his entire life, a great marriage and three loving children, career and financial success and a long life – all were part of this man's improbable and inspirational life.

Papa never lost sight of his mission once he came to the Lord. He was safe and secure in his destiny and wanted everyone to join him. Paul wrote in 2 Timothy 4:7, "I have fought a good fight, I have finished my course, I have kept the faith." God calls us to Him when our mission is finished. Eventually Papa finished the race and was promoted to glory.

Papa is in a better place. John 14:1-3 says:

> "Let not your heart be troubled; ye believe in God; believe also in me. In my Father's house are many mansions; if it were not so, I would have told you. I go to prepare a place for you. And if I go and prepare a place for you, I will come again, and receive you unto myself; that where I am, there ye may be also."

Read those words carefully: "receive you unto myself." That is the goal – to be with Jesus! Papa was the good and faithful servant and now enjoys his eternal reward. Who would have ever thought this possible from where Papa had started or the condition he was in after the war? This story should inspire you to be faithful where you are and trust the Lord to use you in great and mighty ways. When you are, God is even more faithful to the promises in His word. Howard C. Dillaman trusted God and God took that trust and multiplied it through a son who pastors a thriving church and two daughters and their families.

As we enter the final section of this book, I want to share and review the principles and testimonies that were important to Papa in hope that you will be inspired to apply those concepts in your life and walk with the Lord. In many ways, these values are Papa's legacy – the things we remember most and are committed to carry on in his memory – and I hope you will find them important enough to incorporate into your life as well.

Part 3

Papa's Legacy

Chapter 11
Giving

As explained earlier, Papa came from a life of poverty and his work years after the war were a continuation of his early years. One can imagine the challenges of supporting a growing family while selling $39.95 vacuum cleaners door-to-door. Papa never seemed to have any extra money, first experiencing the Depression, later learning how to make counterfeit nickels, then making virtually no money as a soldier and finally serving as a door-to-door salesman. Papa worked hard all hours of the day and night to make ends meet. As a young Christian, however, he had not learned the meaning or importance of giving and the power of offerings. He contributed regularly to the church and charity, but he did not see giving and tithing – which is giving 10% of your income – as part of God's plan.

Eventually, he was in conflict between two concepts as he saw them: providing for his family and God speaking to him about giving back to the Lord. So in 1954 Papa met with the pastor at his church to discuss his concerns about giving. The pastor listened intently and finally told Papa that it was time for him to learn the true meaning of giving back to the Lord, which was giving back to God what already belonged to Him in the first place. He showed Papa in the Bible why the concept of giving was important. Papa prayed with his wife about this and they eventually made tithing a regular part of their lives.

About two years after he began tithing, Papa was once again cashing his paycheck when God spoke to him once more about tithing. Speaking directly to Papa, God said, "Howard, I've blessed you. I want more money. I need more money." Papa interpreted this to mean he must increase his giving to 20%, which he immediately did. All through his working career, Papa gave 20% of his pay to the work of the Lord. What was the result? The Lord blessed him to become one of the top national salesmen in the company. Papa reminded anyone who asked that it was not him but God who produced those great sales achievements. Papa had a wonderful saying, "You don't out-give God. You shovel your money to God and He will shovel it back and use a bigger shovel than you used."

Some years later, Papa and Ethel made a significant financial contribution to the church to fund the acquisition of a new organ. The pastor had shown Papa and his wife how God blesses those who bless Him. From then on, they contributed generously to numerous charitable concerns but the local church was always first.

Tithing is a Christian principle that is often misunderstood by many, even believers. Yet it is easy to do once you come to understand that all things come from and belong to God. God created you and provides for you. You are instructed biblically that you are the custodian of His property. Only through the grace of God do you have what you enjoy and giving acknowledges that fact. When you give you recognize that God is the Giver of what you have and you proclaim that He is able to replenish what you give back to Him. Giving is an ongoing testimony to your faith in God and His ability to provide, not just once or once in a while, but always.

What's more, money can get hold of your heart and mind if you are not careful. Jesus said in Matthew 6:19-21:

> "Do not store up for yourself treasures on earth, where moth and rust destroy and where thieves break in and steal; but store up for yourselves treasures in heaven, where moth and rust do not destroy and where thieves do not break in and steal. For where your treasure is, there your heart will be also."

Michael Youssef, founder and president of "Leading The Way," said on a recent radio broadcast, "Giving is proof that you believe God owns everything!"

Is it any wonder that Papa enjoyed the financial success he did after this? The Bible speaks many times about money – in actuality more than 2,000 times. The Bible is clear as to how money is to be used. Never has there been an era when "self" and "possessions" are more important to folks, including professing Christians. These "things" will not solve the issues of life or make one happy. Yes, maybe for the short term they can satisfy, but eventually you must know your happiness comes from your relationship with the Lord and obedience to His will. Life does not consist of what you have but Who you know.

In 2013, Rock spoke to his congregation that we were near the end of the calendar year and that we must all pray and evaluate our own personal giving back to the Lord as the church's finances were behind budget. I believe this is typical of many churches at the end of their business year. Our church does not often discuss offerings or tithing since there is great confidence among leadership that attenders will respond with their gifts as the year goes along. In this case, however, the deficit was significant so an appeal was made. Rock did not give a twenty-minute sermon or a lecture but rather a brief appeal to return to God what is already His.

A couple of weeks later, Pastor Rock stood before the congregation to report that not only had the deficit been eliminated but also that the response had greatly exceeded the need. As the congregation applauded in joy, Rock read a touching comment written on one of the offering envelopes. That envelope contained 29¢ and was marked "Ninth Street Bridge," and contained a gift by a homeless person in response to the Lord and Rock's appeal. Doesn't this remind one of the story of the widow who gave two small coins during the last week of Jesus' life on earth in Luke 21? Luke 21:3-4 records the words of Jesus: "Of a truth I say unto you, that this poor widow hath cast in more than they all: For all these have their abundance cast in unto the offerings of God: but she of her penury hath cast in all the living that she had." That woman gave from her heart and Jesus noticed it. That small gift of 29¢ was tiny in amount but represented huge faith.

It is my conviction that Rock obtained his faith for finances in part as he grew up watching his father's generosity to the church, charities and to his children. Papa's influence has been multiplied as Rock has taught and led our church. Over the years as I met with Papa, he taught me to appreciate what the Bible had to say about generosity. I had known those principles but not always practiced them. Papa and Rock have helped me do so.

I recently read where many years ago, Michael Benedum, founder of the Claude Worthington Benedum Foundation and a great philanthropist in Pittsburgh, wrote in a codicil to his will and I think it eloquently captures Papa's philosophy where money and wealth were concerned:

> "I have always felt that I have been only a trustee for such material wealth as Providence has placed in my hands. This trusteeship has weighed heavily on me. In carrying out this final responsibility of my stewardship, I have sought to utilize such wisdom and understanding of equity as the Creator has given me. No one with any regard for his responsibility to his God and his fellow man should do less. No one can do more. Only those who sustain the faltering one on the rung above and extend a helping hand to the less fortunate on the rungs below, can approach the end with the strength of sublime faith and confidence."[32]

Michael Benedum, as rich as he was, understood that he was not the source of his financial success but rather it was the Lord Himself.

This statement crystallizes my thinking on how we should think of material wealth. I often hear people say things like "I wish I was rich" or "I wish I would win the lottery." My question to them always is: "What have you done with what God has given you?" The Bible speaks specifically about how God will trust one with much if that person first takes care of a little. Matthew 25:21 teaches, "Well done, thou good and faithful servant; thou hast been faithful over a few things, I will make thee ruler over many things: enter thou into the joy of your Lord."

Tithing as a means of recognizing that God's provision is the source of what we have can be hard to grasp. After all, we all work hard and deserve what we have, right? I may work harder than you so I should have more than you. How can you be so rich when I have so little? We "need" things to show how successful we are. One of the regular things I did with Papa was help him pay his bills. He still owned two apartment buildings when we met so I would review the invoices with Papa, write the checks and then he would sign them. He would always remind me to make a check out for the church if he wasn't putting cash in the offering plate that week.

As a certified public accountant, I prepared Papa's income tax returns and know that Papa gave much more than 10% of his income to the church and others. He also helped many others, very quietly, when the need arose. He would not increase tenants' monthly rent for years, gave coats to the poor and paid for the funeral of friends. Papa would preach messages from 2 Corinthians 3:5: "Not that we are sufficient of ourselves to think anything as of ourselves: but our sufficiency is of God."

Do you have an idol in your life? Is wealth your source of security? Maybe you think wealth will mean God is showing you favor? Abraham in the Old Testament had great wealth – in today's dollars more than the billionaire Warren Buffet currently has. Was wealth his idol? No, his son Isaac was his source of pride. God tested his faith by telling him to give up Isaac. Maybe your idol is relationships, lifestyle, pride or maybe even your own abilities and skill! Are you willing to surrender that idol and trust Jesus? If your idol is money, there is only one way to deal with that and it is through generous giving. Jesus said that when people trust in possessions they create barriers to serving God. Papa did not always understand this and grew in his faith and came to trust God for everything in his life. There is no doubt that Papa's generosity was part of what God used to mold this improbable life from its early shambles.

Papa had acquired moderate wealth as a vacuum cleaner salesman and used those resources to serve the Lord. His wealth did not dictate how he lived his life. I have seen both sides of wealth in my life. I have assisted many families with financial counseling and income tax preparation. I have seen those that are so focused on how they looked, what they drove and where they vacationed that they never repaid their financial debts.

Unfortunately, I have prepared income tax returns for families whose annual income is in excess of $600,000 and they did not return a single dollar to the Lord. How can we be so focused on one's self? Are we that proud? Do we really believe our abundance and success are solely from our own efforts? First Peter 3:3-4 teaches that physical beauty or looks should not be our most noticeable feature. Beauty fades away, but our inner self with a gentle and quiet spirit are worthy in God's sight and generosity is part of that attractive spirit – attractive to the Lord.

Papa tithed, gave above and beyond and instilled the same value in his children. They might or might not have applied it to their lives from time to time, but it wasn't because Papa had not instructed or shown them by example.

So the first legacy value for which we should remember Papa is his generosity and giving. That does not mean this was the most important value, but it was certainly one of the most important to him. If I had to identify his most important, I would think it is what we will discuss in the next chapter and that is Papa's strong drive to share his faith with others.

Chapter 12
Witnessing

In April of 2013, a women named Lois Curry Janke sent Pastor Rock an email. She related that she had seen Rock's title as pastor in a publication and wanted Rock to know that Papa had a major spiritual impact upon her family over the years. Once Rock shared this information with me, I asked him to secure permission for me to interview her by telephone to document the impact to which she was referring. Here is some of the inspiring story she related to me during that interview.

Papa knocked on the door of Mr. and Mrs. George Curry of Cooperstown, Pennsylvania in 1966 when Lois was twenty years old. She related that Papa was as dapper as ever, a perfect gentleman in clothes and in manner. She told me that Papa entered her parents' home and proceeded to tell them about the Electrolux product. Finally, Papa went for the sale by putting some dirt on the floor and demonstrating how efficiently the Electrolux cleaned the floor like no other cleaner could. Lois remembered her parents being impressed and committing to buy one. Papa completed the paperwork and put the finishing touches on the transaction.

During the visit, Papa had determined Mrs. Curry was saved but that George had not come to know the Lord. Papa got on his knees in his nice suit and Lois remembers him saying in a respectful and humble manner, "Now that we have cleaned up your home – let's clean up your lives!" Papa took a Bible out of his business bag and read Scripture to them and prayed with them in their living room. Lois recalled that Papa made such an impact on the entire family that they all owned Electrolux's all of their lives and that his commitment to the Lord was never be forgotten.

Mr. Curry gave his life to the Lord that day. Mr. and Mrs. Curry went on to hold regular Bible studies in their living room on Monday nights and invited all their neighbors. Lois would eventually wed her husband Ron and they would purchase several Electrolux sweepers from Papa, following the example of her parents. Lois felt that Papa sold so many sweepers because people just loved Papa so much! Lois had accepted Jesus Christ as her Savior but her husband, a tough stern man, had not. After a sale of another vacuum to them, Papa turned to Ron and told him that he needed to accept the Lord as his Savior because his wife and children would go to heaven and he would never see them again. Ron accepted Jesus Christ while Papa was still in their home.

Now think for a moment what took place in these two homes. Papa and vacuum cleaners were just tools that God used to proclaim His name. Papa was so confident in his faith that he was just not willing, but in a sense driven, to proclaim Jesus Christ as his Savior. He did not care if he lost the sale of the cleaner because he wasn't just selling cleaners. He was helping save sinners. Now just because Papa proceeded in this manner does not mean that you and I must tell the world of Jesus Christ in the same way. That is the point. Every person in every situation is a potential opportunity to share God's love to another – maybe through a good deed, with a loving smile, in praying for and with someone, in the delivery of a meal for the poor or sick or in going on a missions trip. There are endless ways to bring the good news of salvation to others. May we in our faith be as bold as Papa was in his.

One morning while praying, God again spoke to Papa, instructing him to write a gospel tract. After first ignoring this voice of God, he was again instructed to prepare this tract. Eventually Papa followed those instructions. He sat down with paper and pencil and wrote the tract as God spoke to him. The first printing was 500 pieces. He used photographs of his family and a message of the need for salvation. He never updated the photos over the years, much to the chagrin of his children. He told me he had 5,000 printed at a time and had distributed over 50,000 in his lifetime with the same photographs and the same message!

The Schaffner Printing Company in Butler, Pennsylvania did the printing. The company was founded by Eugene Schaffner, Sr. in 1954. Papa became one of his largest customers with that unique printing job. The founder's grandson, James Schaffner, runs the business today after taking over from his father in 1979. He told me the booklets would have cost about $.12 each back in the 1950s but that it was unlikely Papa paid for the booklets. He related that his father often bartered printing jobs for items they needed and they surely needed a vacuum cleaner. James remembers growing up with only Electrolux vacuum cleaners in their home, just like his grandfather's home.

James has quite a memory. He related that he attended Butler Senior High School with Papa's children and that my wife, Vicki, was a classmate. I told him I was married to Vicki and he said, "I was in the band with her. She was pretty so they put her up front. The less attractive girls were asked to play the flute. I should know since I was playing the tuba in the back." That was a funny conversation. I let him know that Victoria was still very attractive.

Papa's booklet *Life's Greatest Concern*

You can see at the end of this book how to order your own copy of this amazing little booklet, but let me here provide for you each and every word Papa shared with the unsaved in that little tract:

LIFE'S GREATEST CONCERN

Life's Greatest Concern is not Pleasure

Life's Greatest Concern is not Success

Life's Greatest Concern is not Health

Life's Greatest Concern is not Wealth

Life's Greatest Concern is not Education

Life's Greatest Concern is -

Where will you spend eternity?

One of two places awaits you - mansions with God (John 14:2) or torment forever with the devil (Luke 16:23). To spend eternity with God, you must be born again (John 3:3) and you must be converted (Matt 18:3). To spend eternity with the devil, do nothing, stay just as you are - a sinner! "For all have sinned and come short of the Glory of God" (Rom 3:23). "For the wages of sin is death: but the gift of God is eternal life through Jesus Christ, our Lord" (Rom 6:23).

YOUR PART

"Repent and be converted that your sins be blotted out" (Acts 3:19). "Except Ye repent (turn from sin) Ye shall all likewise perish" (Luke 13:3). Confess your Sins to Jesus - "For there is one God, and one mediator between God and Men, the Man Christ Jesus" (1 Timothy 2:5).

DO IT NOW!

"Behold now is the day of salvation" (2 Corinthians 6:2).

How shall we escape if we neglect so great salvation (Hebrews 2:3).

RESULTS

"Therefore, if any man be in Christ he is a new creature: Old things are passed away, behold, all things are become new" (2 Corinthians 5:17).

"What shall it profit a man if he gain the whole world and lose his own soul?" (Mark 8:36).

REMINDER!

Every one of us shall give account of himself to God.

CONFESSSION

Being convinced that I am a lost sinner and knowing that "Christ died for me," I NOW accept him as my Savior. With his help I am willing to turn from my sin and confess Him before men.

SIGNED ________________________________

Those are perfect words, aren't they? They are words inspired by a life committed to live for the Lord, words that everyone needs to hear and not be afraid to share with others. It seems that rejection never concerned Papa. Notice the final line where he asked for a signature! Papa was indicating to his readers that this was a real commitment, not just for a moment but forever! He was going to make every attempt, either through the booklet or his testimony if he met you out walking or at a place like a convention. Papa was going to tell you about his Lord no matter where you were or he was at the time. Any moment might be the right one to lead someone to the Lord and an everlasting life. "Come to the Lord Jesus Christ and be saved or suffer the consequences" – his message was that simple.

Papa would walk up to a total stranger and just say, "Have I ever given you a copy of my book?" If they said, "No," he would seize the opportunity to introduce himself and his Savior and hand them a booklet. It was just that simple and non-threatening. We were at McDonald's one day for our regular weekly burger when he asked an employee behind the counter the magic question. When he got a "no," Papa proudly proclaimed that the person behind the counter was person number 50,001 to receive his little book. It was as if both of them had won a major prize.

Was Papa brash? No, I don't think so, but he was persistent and confident in what he was doing. Papa was never afraid to speak about Christ because he knew his subject matter. His pockets always had booklets so that an opportunity to tell someone about Jesus would not escape him. I am proud to say that, like many family members, I have given the booklet to my family members and friends, and I always share the story of why and how the booklet came about. There is no telling how many have come to the Lord as a result of Papa's book or his testimonies. I am confident that many now know Jesus Christ because of Papa and that booklet. That was such a small booklet with a large message, a message that has stood the test of time.

Papa did not take for granted that anyone was saved, regardless of their position in life. He knew just because folks were in church did not mean they knew Christ and were "born again." He asked people if they knew Jesus regardless of how "saved" they looked. One time Papa asked a Presbyterian pastor that very question while delivering a vacuum cleaner to the church. Can you imagine that? I can see him asking that question of many people in his daily journey. But to ask the church pastor?

Well, God works in mysterious ways. The pastor responded, "I do not understand what that means." Papa seized the moment, praying with him and leading him to a true relationship with the Lord. After this special experience, the pastor asked Papa to preach to his congregation, relating that he himself could not. Papa might have been a vacuum cleaner salesman but he was first and foremost an instrument of God. He preached to that church and as many as one-half of those in attendance accepted Jesus Christ as their Lord and Savior that night. Then they knew what it meant to be "born again."

There are many other examples of Papa sharing his testimony in unlikely situations. One I recall involved him attending another convention, this one in Boca Raton, Florida. As Papa boarded the plane in Pittsburgh, he took his seat along with his wife Ethel in the rear section of the aircraft. It was the only place he would sit as he felt if there were a plane crash, only those in the tail section would survive. During the course of the flight, after serving all of the passengers with food and refreshments, the young flight attendant sat down in the only seat available, which was next to Papa. As she picked up a pocket novel she had brought with her, Papa handed her one of his tracts and said, "Here, would you read this instead?" She took it and started to read it. Papa noticed a tear in her eye so he asked her, "Do you know Jesus?" She paused for a moment and said, "Mister, I've been an atheist all of my life."

Then she said, "This is the strangest day of my life. Something has been bothering me for two or three weeks and I didn't know what it was until I read your book and it told me. I'm lost." Papa had her slide over closer to him, took a pocket Bible out of his jacket and read her Romans 3:23. "For the wages of sin is death: but the gift of God is eternal life through Jesus Christ our Lord." He then turned to Romans 5:8, "But God commended his love toward us, in that, while we were yet sinners, Christ died for us."

"Did you know that someone suffered and died for you?" Papa asked her.

She responded, "I didn't know anything about that, but how can I be changed?"

Papa related, "By asking God into your heart and confessing your sins."

"I can't in front of all of these people on this plane," she told him.

Papa informed her, "Jesus died in front of a lot of people for you."

With that, she dropped down on her knees and she cried out to God to save her. Papa noted that she got off the plane with the biggest smile he had ever seen. Two weeks later, Papa got a letter from Omaha, Nebraska. It said, "I am the young stewardess that you led to Christ on that plane. Thank you for being on that plane. What a life I've gotten. My life has been changed, just because you were on that airplane." Papa would say there was no greater joy then leading someone to Jesus Christ.

Because Papa had become such a successful salesman, he was often asked to speak at the national conventions about his strategy for sales success. On the same trip that Papa led the stewardess to the Lord, he was asked to speak at the convention. It would be attended by all of the "big-wigs" as Papa would call them. They would come from all over the United States, Europe and Canada. Papa noted that most religious persuasions were represented (Catholics, Protestants, Jews, atheists, agnostics) and that the only time you heard of God was in a curse word. Three top salesmen (from 18,000 total) were seated with their wives in the front row, waiting to speak.

While seated, God spoke to Papa, "Howard, when you get up there, I want you to tell them about Jesus and not vacuum cleaners!" Papa said his knees began to shake, as the 5,000 people there came to hear about vacuum cleaners and not Jesus Christ. Papa turned to his wife and said, "When I get up there, I'm going to witness for Christ!"

Ethel stated, "Don't you dare. They'll throw you out."

Papa quickly said, "They can't throw me out. I'm one of the top salesmen in the United States." The other two salesmen spoke for about seven minutes each, sharing their sales tactics that had made them successful. Papa finally took the stage and as he put it, he upset the applecart. He never ever said a single word about vacuum cleaners! When he finished, he was taken to an office in Boca Raton where his presentation was copied, put in a magazine and sent to 500 newspapers in the United States and Canada.

What had Papa said? What was his testimony? Papa was not beyond creating a story to get his point across, and that day told of a young boy named "Billy." Billy was picked on and made fun of by the local boys in the neighborhood. One boy in particular was especially mean. He played dirty tricks on Billy and made his life miserable. This boy was the son of a local physician and was perhaps jealous since Billy was a good kid. Well, one day, this boy became terribly ill and his life was saved due to Billy donating some organs for a transplant. Papa used that story to demonstrate God's love for us, in spite of how unworthy we are. The analogy was that Jesus Christ (Billy), although mistreated, died for us on the cross for each and every one of us. My wife Victoria had heard this story so many times that only later in life did she learn that "Billy" did not actually exist as a real person.

Papa led the lost to the Lord by teaching the Bible and praising the Lord. He never lost sight of the mission. It was not to make money or to get attention. It was to proclaim

Jesus Christ as the Savior and the need to acknowledge our sinful nature and ask for forgiveness. Papa used John 3:16 as an important part of his message: "For God so loved the world that He gave His only begotten Son, that whosoever believeth in Him should not perish, but have everlasting life." Papa never rested on his accomplishments. He would also use Philippians 3:13-14 in his presentations:

> "Brothers, I do not consider myself yet to have apprehended: but this one thing I do, forgetting those things which are behind, and reaching forth, unto those things which are before, I press toward the mark for the prize of the high calling of God in Christ Jesus."

Papa was a constant witness for the Lord. In Acts 1:1-11 before Jesus ascended to Heaven, He instructed His disciples on what they should do. Verse eight says, "But you will receive power, when the Holy Spirit comes on you; and you will be my witnesses in Jerusalem, and in all Judea and in Samaria, and to the ends of the earth." Part of witnessing is learning to take up your own cross and follow Jesus. Papa realized it was ceasing to make one's own self the center of attention. The words of Jesus in Mark 8:34-36 teach us,

"Whosoever will come after me, let him deny himself, and take up his cross, and follow me. For whosoever will save his life shall lose it; but whosoever shall lose his life for my sake and the gospel's, the same shall save it. For what shall it profit a man, if he shall gain the whole world, and lose his own soul?"

Melissa Pearce, President of Enduring Hope Ministries, put it this way:

> "It's about bringing glory and honor to the One who paid the ultimate price for our freedom. Jesus displayed a heart of complete surrender to God the Father. He literally took up His Cross to walk in obedience to the Father's will. Just as the cross led to His death for our sins, we will symbolically carry our own cross, meaning total commitment to Christ Jesus no matter the cost."[33]

Dwight L. Moody, the great American evangelist, said, "We are told to let our light shine, and if it does, we won't need to tell anybody it does. Lighthouses don't fire cannons to call attention to their shining – they just shine." We all need to witness and shine for the Lord. Keep in mind that we never know when our witness will impact a life. Every experience is a potential opportunity to show God's love. Papa knew this and trained his children to know the same. The following is an example of how Papa's example impacted and directed my wife's life at one point.

Victoria was a talent acquisition specialist (recruiter) for a large bank in the Pittsburgh region. She spent hours on the telephone and Internet filling needed positions for the bank. Recently she was talking with a potential candidate. In the conversation it came out that my wife had lost her son Hill several years ago when he was 28 years old. The candidate asked how she had survived from day-to-day from such a tragedy. Victoria related that it was not easy "But through the grace of Jesus Christ, I will go forward. My son is with Christ today." Sharing our trust in the Lord is so important. Some today have no sense of God and instead are looking for worldly answers to their problems.

Four days later, my wife was informed that the candidate would not be coming to Pittsburgh on Tuesday for her initial interview. Her son had been in a vehicle accident over the weekend and died. Victoria reached out to make contact with her and assist her in any way possible. Victoria and I discussed the incident and were trusting that Victoria's witnessing would help the candidate to find peace in a very difficult situation. On Thursday, she called Victoria in tears. She had buried her son and wanted to tell Victoria that she was now her best friend.

She stated, "God put you in my path. Thank you so much." Though stunned by the loss of her child, she noted that great things would come from his life. He had been an organ donor and his heart, kidneys, corneas and skin would help 40-50 people. We never know when witnessing will touch a life! It was not a coincidence that this took place. God touched her life hours before the tragic event. God put Victoria and her testimony in that woman's path.

With my father passing away at a young age, my grandmother would speak of how painful it was to bury a child. My mother spoke of the same thing when my brother was stillborn and another brother died young from cancer. Victoria had suffered through the loss of her son. One day at church, I was sharing these events with one of our staff pastors and his response impacted me. He said, "These events are terrible and painful but just imagine how God must have felt when He sent His Son to carry the burden of sin for the entire world. His agonizing death on the cross would be an ultimately brutal death of a child."

Papa witnessed to thousands in his lifetime but none was probably more important to Papa than his father. His dad had never came to know the Lord but Papa witnessed to him his entire life and finally, on his death bed at age 86, Papa's father accepted Jesus Christ as his Lord and Savior with Papa at his side.

Many feel the Lord's coming is near. Of course, none of us know when that will happen. He is waiting to give everyone an opportunity to come to him. We are specifically instructed in the Bible to witness to others. Jesus said, as recorded in Matthew 28:19-20:

> "Go ye therefore, and teach all nations, baptizing them in the name of the Father and of the Son and of the Holy Ghost; teaching them to observe all things whatsoever I have commanded you: and lo, I am with you always, even unto the very end of the world."

Papa lived his life with these verses in his heart. What is the condition of your heart? Aleksandr Solzhenitsyn wrote in *Gulag Archipelago* while in Soviet prison, "That the line separating good and evil passes not through states, not through classes, not through political parties, but right through every human heart."[34] All of us have things in our heart we need to fix but we are powerless to do so. The heart was described by C.S. Lewis in *Surprised by Joy* as "a zoo of lusts, a bedlam of ambitions, a nursery of fears, a harem of fondled hatreds."[35] God is at work in the lives of all willing people – changing and transforming them into more than they were. Max Anders said, "The gospel is carried to imperfect people by imperfect people. Then these imperfect people are to band together to help one another grow to spiritual maturity, warts and all."[36]

Papa brought God's message to everyone's heart. That message was the source of his improbable life and Papa wanted to share that life with as many others as possible before he went to meet His Maker. It's important to note, however, that his improbable life would have never occurred if not for a group of men we will discuss in the next chapter.

Chapter 13
The Bible and Church

It should be no surprise that Papa, who came to know the Lord through his encounter with a Bible in his VA hospital room, remained a "man of the Word" for the remainder of his days. The Bible became Papa's guidebook for faith and life. When I heard that Papa came to the Lord by first reading a Gideon's Bible, it got me thinking about the organization. I was aware of their Bibles, seeing them many times while traveling, but knew little else, so I decided to do some research.

The Gideons International was founded in 1899 and served as an extended missionary arm of the church. It is the oldest association of Christian businessmen and professional men in the U.S. Gideons first forced through unusual circumstances. John H. Nicholson of Janesville, Wisconsin, came to the Central Hotel in Boscobel, Wisconsin, for a night of rest. The hotel was crowded and they suggested he take a bed in a double room with Samuel E. Hill, of Beloit, Wisconsin. The two men discovered they both were Christians and held their evening devotions together. On their knees before God a relationship was fostered that later developed into an association.

On May 31, 1899, the two men met again at Beaver Dam, Wisconsin, where they concluded to band together Christian commercial travelers for mutual recognition, personal evangelism and united service for the Lord. They decided to call a meeting in Janesville, Wisconsin on July 1, 1899 at the local Y.M.C.A. Only three men were present at that meeting – John H. Nicholson, Samuel E. Hill and William J. Knights. They organized with Hill as the president, Knights as vice president, and Nicholson as secretary and treasurer. Much thought was given to what the name of the association should be, and after special prayer that God might lead them to select the proper name, Mr. Knights arose from his knees and said, "We shall be called Gideons." He read the sixth and seventh chapters of Judges that showed the reason for adopting that name. Gideon, which means "destroyer" or "mighty warrior" in Hebrew, was a judge of the Hebrews as told in Judges 6. As is the pattern throughout the book of Judges, the Israelites regularly turned away from God after years of peace and were consequently oppressed by the neighboring Midianites and Amalekites. In one instance God chose Gideon, a young man from the tribe of Manasseh, to free the people of Israel from the Midianites and to condemn their worship of idols.

In view of the fact that almost all of the Gideons in the early years of the association were traveling men, the question quite naturally arose regarding how they might be more effective witnesses in the hotels where they spent much of their time. One trustee went so far as to suggest that the Gideons furnish a Bible for each bedroom of every hotel in the United States. He commented, "In my opinion, this would not only stimulate the activities of the rank and file of the membership but would be a gracious act, wholly in keeping with the divine mission of the Gideon Association." The plan, which they called "The Bible Project" was adopted at Louisville, Kentucky in 1908.[37]

It has been more than 100 years since Gideons International placed the first Bible in a hotel room in Montana. Today Gideons have chapters in more than 190 countries around the globe. Bibles and New Testaments are printed for distribution in at least 90 languages. In the past, students in the fifth grade and above were given Bibles and New Testaments. Modern society has decided to keep those Bibles out of the schools but the Gideons did not give up. Starting in 2009, the Gideons produced *The Life Book* with the goal of putting one in the hands of every high school student. This book tells God's story, includes quotes from the Bible and addresses common faith questions that younger folks may be struggling with. Praise the Lord for this thoughtful and effective method to combat the world's attempts to limit or extinguish God's word. For more information on this movement, one can go to www.thelifebook.com or to www.gideons.org.

It was through this "Bible Project" that Papa was first exposed to the word of God. Religion had never been part of his life but God had been watching over and protecting him his entire life. I know you can see how subtly this took place. Papa was ill, downtrodden and alone. His mind had not been clear and he was physically spent. God put him in a small room that contained a small book that would change Papa's life along with the lives of thousands of others. God can work in your life in many not-so-obvious ways. Not everything is a lightning bolt, a burning bush or the parting of the Red Sea. In fact, most of those life-changing experiences are not like that at all. We must be ready and open to receiving God's direction for our lives in gentle ways that are easy to pass by.

I have often told Papa's story to friends and anyone who would listen. They were always amazed by his story and I love telling it. I told the story to my good friend, Jim Morey, in Savannah, Georgia. We had been neighbors for many years in Lancaster County, Pennsylvania and he now resides in the South. He told me one of his fellow church members was involved in the Gideons and Jim was sure he would love to hear Papa's story.

So I reproduced the article about Papa that had appeared in the *Pittsburgh Post-Gazette*. I forwarded it to Jim, who then gave it to John Gandy, the Gideons' member and a true Southern gentleman. Mr. Gandy presented it to the Gideons' leadership and Papa's story was eventually told at a Gideons' national convention in Atlanta, Georgia. Mr. Gandy has used Papa's story many times since learning of it. Jim saw Mr. Gandy at church recently and asked him if he had told the Howard Dillaman testimony lately. His response was, "Are you kidding? Of course I have. Howard Dillaman is my 'go to' story."

Once Papa came to know the Lord, he also became a

"church man" as well as a man of the Word. Church became a regular and important part of his life. He did not originally attend a Christian and Missionary Alliance (C&MA) church. He attended another Christian denomination's local church in the Butler area. As explained earlier, Papa felt the church was not as Bible-oriented and mission-driven as he felt it needed to be, so he sought a new church home. This is important. If you are not being properly fed the gospel of Jesus Christ, you need to make a change. A church is a place to worship God, sing His praises and fellowship with believers. We all need good Bible teaching, the presence of the Spirit, and community love.

Here is a little about the C&MA denomination that I discovered through research. Founded by Rev. Albert B. Simpson in 1887, a Presbyterian clergyman from Canada, the C&MA is a Jesus-centered, evangelical Protestant denomination. Simpson witnessed the physical and spiritual plight of New York City's homeless, downtrodden and marginalized population. Moved by his love for Christ and lost people, Simpson devoted his life to sharing Jesus' light – in word and deed – with the city and ultimately the nations. He believed Christ was not only his Savior, but also his Sanctifier, through a dramatic spiritual encounter that changed the course of his life. He also experienced Christ as his Healer after struggling with poor health for years.

He was compelled by a sense of urgency to take this message to all nations because of Jesus' statement in Matthew 24:14: "And this gospel of the kingdom shall be preached in all the world for a witness unto all nations;

and then shall the end come." Simpson established the New York Gospel Tabernacle to bring likeminded people together into an organization that could facilitate outreach ministries. He also set up the Missionary Training Institute (MTI) to provide training and resources for men and women God was calling to take the gospel to the world. During those early years, Simpson's group sent out the first team of missionaries to the Congo. Since then, thousands of people have followed God's call to serve him through the C&MA in the United States and abroad.

The Christian and Missionary Alliance was formed as a missionary society, not a denomination. The early congregations were called "branches," which were formed to promote missionary endeavors and the "deeper life" (focusing on Christ our Sanctifier). The "branches" usually met on Sunday afternoons, so that people could attend their denominational church's worship service on Sunday mornings. People who attended these "branches" came from most of the major denominations. In time as mainline denominations became increasingly liberal in their doctrine, these "branches" began to operate like churches and were organized as such. It was not until 1974 that an official C&MA denomination was formed. Current worldwide membership is more than five million people with more than 2,000 churches in the United States. Prominent C&MA members include author A.W. Tozer and Evangelist Billy Graham, who preached his first sermons as a licensed youth pastor in a C&MA church.

The C&MA denomination offices formerly were

located in Nyack, New York, which continues to be the home for Nyack College and the Alliance Theological Seminary. The headquarters, however, are now located in Colorado Springs, Colorado. The C&MA wholeheartedly serves God and the people of the world, basing their work solely on the Bible. They live and die by the words of the Bible and believe they bring the only life worth living – one wholly committed to the King Jesus.

Papa faithfully served and supported his local church in Butler. While he was not permitted to serve as an elder due to his divorce from his first wife who abandoned their marriage (the C&MA has since changed that restriction for similar situations), he served in every other capacity. As mentioned earlier, he also supported the church with finances and his presence.

Papa knew that Jesus died to build the Church and he had an obligation to love what Jesus loved. That is important, for today many say, "I love Jesus but don't like the Church." Pastor Rock one time said in a sermon, "You can't say to God, I love you and but hate your bride. No husband on earth would tolerate that kind of relationship and God won't either!" If you have been hurt in a church, then the answer isn't to sit at home. It's time to find another church! Of course Papa's love for the church was rewarded when Rock became a pastor and Papa spoke in many churches to help build up the members and lead others to Christ. Papa was a Bible-man and a Church-man.

In my mind, these last chapters summarize Papa's legacy – his generosity, his witnessing and his commitment to family, the Word and the Church. As you know by now, Papa was a man of the Word and a man of words, since he witnessed and spoke before groups so often. In my research of his life and in looking through his Bible, I have recovered and uncovered many things that he said, things that God used to inspire others as Papa shared them. I thought it would be appropriate to share those things with you so you can feel the effect that those words had on others – and will hopefully have on you. So as we close out this book on this improbable life, let's take a look at some of Papa's favorite verses and sayings.

Chapter 14
Some Sayings to Help Remember Papa

Three things drove me to write this book: my firm conviction that Papa's improbable and inspiring life path needed to be told; my desire to give Papa's little witnessing booklet a new lease on life; and my hope that his story would inspire you to find and fulfill your story in Christ. What better way to end this book than by sharing some of the quotes, comments and phrases written in Papa's Bible and his witnessing notes? I include many of his quotes, comments, favorite passages and readings in this chapter, with additional items listed in the Appendix. All these little nuggets, so carefully preserved in a Bible, are more aspects of Papa's life that so endeared him to me. Papa's Bible is remarkable to look through, read and reflect. Not only does it contain the word of God but also a running history of Papa's life and insight is written in the margins.

Papa read and studied his Bible daily, sometimes several times a day. Papa knew it was the infallible, inspired Word of God and a reliable guide in all life matters. Psalm 19:7 says, "The law of the Lord is perfect, converting the soul; the testimony of the Lord is sure, making wise the simple." Proverbs 30:5 states, "Every word of God is pure; he is a shield unto them that put their trust in him." Papa knew that the Bible is the whole truth and free from error for God cannot lie. "God is not a man, that he should lie; neither the son of man, that he should repent" (Numbers 23:19). Papa made a commitment to read the entire Bible annually ,and at his death the yearly streak was 32 years and counting.

Papa's Bible

Papa owned many Bibles, but like his wallet and sweaters he found no need to change from the old one which worked just fine. Three black stripes of electrical tape – two inches wide and fourteen inches long – held it together. There is not a topic in the Bible about which he did not have notes and comments written. The Trinity, being born again, assurance, salvation, the second coming, temptation, heaven and hell were subjects Papa studied and preached about.

Papa knew that heaven was the ultimate reward but the journey there began with the journey here on earth. Papa also knew the terrible destiny for those that did not come to the Lord. Do you think you know the way to the Lord? Many think they do but they will be sadly mistaken. We have become familiar with the comments: "Oh, I was a good person, I never killed anybody!" "I go to church every week." "I did lots of good deeds."

There is more to getting into heaven than charity or being nice. One must be clear in understanding the path to heaven. In John 14:6, Jesus says, "I am the way, the truth, and the life: no man cometh unto the Father, but by me." Romans 10:9 tells us, "If thou shalt confess with thy mouth the Lord Jesus, and shalt believe in thine heart that God hath raised him from the dead, thou shalt be saved." We are born in sin and must accept Jesus Christ as the Savior who paid the price of our sins on the cross. There is *no other way!*

Papa professed Jesus Christ because he knew that when Christ returns in glory, the spirit of the age will be silenced once and for all and that everyone will bow to the

Papa's Bible with notes

Lordship of Jesus Christ. There will then be no doubt as to who is the King of kings and Lord of lords. He wanted even more hearts to celebrate and rejoice before the throne of Jesus Christ.

The New York Times publishes a list of bestselling books every week and gives special attention to the top ten. Did you ever notice that the Bible is not listed, yet continues to be the bestselling book of all time? They do not put the Bible on the list because nothing else would ever make the top of the list. It is estimated that over six billion Bibles have been printed and distributed (I don't know who did the estimating) and it has been translated into more than 1,300 languages and dialects. Papa knew it from cover to cover. A.W. Tozer in his book *The Pursuit of God* wrote regarding the Bible, "I think a new world will arise out of the religious mists when we approach our Bible with the idea that it is not only a Book which was once spoken, but a Book which is now speaking."[38]

Let's end by viewing some of the notes in Papa's Bible. Keep in mind they were written by a man that did not engage God or His Word until later in life. Because he trusted the Lord when God spoke to him, however, Papa became a warrior for his God. Let Papa be the example that no matter how tough times get, no matter how it seems God does not care about us, accept by faith the fact that He does! Bring Christ into your life today! Here are some of Papa's quotes and key life verses:

"Any dead fish can float with the current. It takes a ***live*** fish to swim against the current to goodness."

"Jesus Christ paid a debt he did not owe for a debt we could not pay: Forgiveness"

"Nothing but the blood of Jesus."

"The church is God's recovery program."

"Some people never look up (to God) until they are lying on their back."

"Prayer is the Christian's greatest weapon."

"The Bible will keep you from sin or sin will keep you from the Bible."

"If you were arrested for being a Christian, would they have enough evidence to convict you?"

"If you must gossip, gossip the Bible."

"You have never done anything worth remembering in life until you can remember when you won a soul to Jesus Christ."

"Satan deceives you but God tells you the truth."

"You might reject and dislike a doctor's diagnosis, but that does not change the facts; same with accepting Jesus Christ. The facts are heaven and hell."

"No one can say God is unfair in permitting a sinner to go to hell. We all deserve hell."

"The sinner would give a million worlds to go back and relive his life, but his die is cast, it is to hell."

"Don't look at your children as an inconvenience but as God's potential."

"I am so glad I am part of the family of God."

"I can count on him. Can he count on you?"

"We pray for things God knows before we ask for what we need."

"He came to be like us so we could become like Him."

"Baptism is good but when it becomes a substitute for salvation, it is tragic."

God sends no one to hell. You must:

Climb over the body of Christ;
Climb over the Word of God;
Climb over all who have prayed for you;
Climb over the church building.

TO GET TO HELL!

"I present to you Jesus Christ, not for debate but for decision."

"God gave us 10 commandments, not suggestions!"

"When Satan reminds you of your past, remind Satan of his future!"

"Christ died for you – what have you done for him?"

"Christianity is a religion of Songs – All of the 'isms' have no songs."

"For all have sinned and come short of the glory of God" (Romans 3:23).

"Believe on the Lord Jesus Christ and thou shalt be saved" (Acts 16:31).

"For by grace are ye saved through faith; and that not of yourselves; it is the gift of God; not of works, lest any man should boast" (Ephesians 2:8-9).

"It's hard to think about heaven's message when our minds are filled with worldly static."

"Be so good you can't be ignored."

"Never doubt in the dark what God has told you in the light."

"One drink can't hurt you. One cigarette can't hurt you. A little swear word didn't hurt. Little did you realize that little but sinful pleasures would multiply into many sinful pleasures and cause total destruction to your soul."

"God allows the storm to teach us."

"Satan is real – like a lion trying to devour us and destroy your effectiveness for God."

"How they will know you love me – how much you love on another."

"Let your conversation be without covetousness; be content with such things as ye have; for he hath said, 'I will never leave thee, nor forsake thee'" (Hebrews 13:5).

"You will seek me and find me, when ye shall search for me with all your heart. And I will be found by you, saith the Lord" (Jeremiah 29:13-14a).

"God doesn't call those that are equipped – he equips those that he calls."

"God allows pain to humble us – to show us how much we need him."

"If thou shalt confess with thy mouth the Lord Jesus, and shalt believe in thine heart that God hath raised him from the dead, thou shalt be saved" (Romans 10:9).

"For by grace are ye saved through faith; and that not of yourselves: it is the gift of God: Not of works, lest any man should boast" (Ephesians 2: 8-9).

"Enter not into the path of the wicked, and go not in the way of evil men. Avoid it, pass not by it, turn from it, and pass away" (Proverbs 4:14-15).

"If we confess our sins, he is faithful and just to forgive

us our sins and to cleanse us from all unrighteousness" (1 John 1:9).

"In the beginning was the Word and the Word was with God, and the Word was God. The same was in the beginning with God. All things were made by him; and without him was not anything made that was made" (John 1:1-3).

"Though he were a Son, yet learned he obedience by the things which he suffered" (Hebrews 5: 8).

"How important to us it is to express our appreciation to our Lord for what he did for us."

"God promised a safe landing – not smooth sailing!"

"People who ask questions of the right people get the right answers" - Douglas MacArthur.

"Life is like a tea bag. You never know how strong it is until you are put into hot water."

"You love the Jesus you cannot see by loving those you can see."

"If God be for us, who can be against us?" (Romans 8:31).

"Trust in yourself, and you are doomed to be disappointed; Trust in your friends, and they will die and leave you; Trust in money, and you may have it taken from you; Trust in reputation, and some slanderous tongue may blast it; But TRUST IN GOD, and you are never to be confounded in time or eternity" - D. L. Moody.

I think you get the idea by now that I consider Papa a remarkable man. His story, words and example deeply impacted my life. I have done my best to share those things with you in the hope that they will impact your life as well. This book started with Papa's funeral but ends as I described his legacy as it lives on through his family and the thousands of people he personally touched. Now that you have read this book, I hope you can be added to the list of those who have been touched by his story.

It would give Papa great pleasure not to know that a book was written about him, but that God used a book written about him for God's purpose and glory. Knowing that for a fact, I commit this work to God's care and pray that He will use it to move you and many others to find purpose in Christ and healing from pain. Papa lived an improbable life and you can too. I hope this book will inspire you to do so.

Acknowledgements

Never in my life did I ever think I would write a book. My greatest concern was and is that I did Papa's story justice. In the process, I take responsibility for any mistakes I might have made. I tried my best to verify the facts and keep my interpretation to a minimum. The Holy Spirit walked with me through this entire project. I am so grateful that Jesus put Papa into my life path. As I wrote this book I cannot tell you how inspired I have been by researching, interviewing and reading about Papa. It has taken me deeper into the Bible and enriched my prayer life. It has caused me to cry as I remembered him, but it comforts me that, like my own immediate family, I will see him again in heaven.

I want to first thank my lovely bride, **Victoria**. I love you! This has not been an easy experience for her. My constantly asking questions for clarification of events would often cause her to reflect upon a father she greatly misses. Yet she would always assist me, often reminiscing about an experience with her Dad. She has wholeheartedly supported me and she also feels strongly that Papa's legacy must continue.

My thanks to **Cindy Rago, Debbie Kailer** and **Peter Grewar**. I am appreciative of your proofing and editing skills. I could not have moved forward without you. To **Rock, Karen** and the other family members, I will always be indebted for the time you committed to helping me get my facts correct. To Congressman and friend **Mike Kelly** and staffer **Jennifer Pontzer,** your help in securing documents from the Veteran's Administration was invaluable. To **John Stanko,** your ability and expertise to actually publish a book is greatly appreciated. Thank you for your guidance and encouragement. I will be forever grateful for your counsel. Your love for the Lord has added so much to this project.

To my friend of more than thirty years, **Jim Morey,** who has been an endless source of encouragement and help. Your introduction to **John Gandy** brought the Gideons International experiences so close. And your Christian example through the years has helped me as I have raised my children.

Finally, I dedicate this book to my children, **Christopher and Anne Marie**, my brother **David** and my parents, **Maurice and Patricia Peuler**. David coached me along the way and was so looking forward to the publication of the book but the Lord called him home before it was completed. And to Christopher and Anne Marie, I love you dearly. I know I have not always been the best example as a father and Christian. I trust this book will encourage you that, as Papa has shown, no matter how difficult our journey, our Lord Jesus Christ loves us and has His hand on His children at all times; knowing that we can and must lead others to the Lord through our witness and words. And to Mom and Dad, you raised us all in a Christian home, never compromising your faith. You taught us the godly way. I am forever grateful.

Appendix 1

Here are a few more things that were written inside Papa's Bible. I guess he used that as we use computer files today!

Baby-manger - 2,000 years ago

Lived only 33 years - name never forgotten

Great men have been forgotten

Tabernacles, cathedrals and churches cost billions of dollars

Every Sunday millions worship him

Give millions of dollars every year

Millions of songs written in his name

Thousands of books written

Sermons preached every week

Radio & TV seven days a week

Missionaries go all over the world

Men travel throughout the world

Baptism in his name

Live by his name

Die rather than deny his name

Millions pray to his name every day

He healed the sick

Opened the eyes of the blind

Made the lame walk

Cleansed the leper - cast out demons

Raised the dead

Fed 5,000

Calmed the sea

Walked on water

Healed the broken hearted

Comforted the lonely

Transformed lives of the sinful

Some said he was a prophet

Some said a teacher

Some said just a man

If so, he must have had an awfully good advertising agent

to keep his name alive 2,000 years

Yes, he was all that, but

more than that, he was

the Son of God

The Clock of Life

The clock of life is wound but once,

And no man has the power

To tell just when the hands will stop

At late or early hour.

To lose one's wealth is bad indeed.

To lose one's health is more.

To lose one's soul is such a loss

That no man can restore.

The present only is our own.

Live, Love, toil with a will.

Place no faith in 'tomorrow'

for the clock may then be still

"39 people died while you read this short poem. Every hour 5,417 go to meet their Maker. You could have been among them. Are you ready?"[39]

How The 15 Disciples Died For Witnessing

Matthew was slain with a sword.

Mark died being dragged through
the streets of Alexandria.

Luke was hanged on an olive tree in Greece.

John was thrown into a cauldron of boiling oil.

Peter was crucified upside down in Rome.

James was beheaded in Jerusalem.

James the Less was thrown from a high pinnacle and
beaten to death with a club.

Philip was hanged.

Bartholomew was scourged and beaten till he died.

Andrew was bound to a cross and preached at the top of
his voice to his persecutors till he died.

Thomas' body was run through with a lance.

Jude was killed by arrows shot by his executioners.

Matthias was stoned and beheaded.

Barnabas was stoned to death at Salonica.

Paul was tortured and then beheaded in Rome.

Papa loved this piece and used it often in his messages:

FOOTPRINTS

By Mary Stevenson

One night a man had a dream. He dreamed he was walking along the beach with the Lord. Across the sky flashed scenes from his life. For each scene, he noticed two sets of footprints in the sand; one belonged to him, and the other to the Lord.

When the last scene of his life flashed before him, he looked back at the footprints in the sand. He noticed that many times along the path of his life there was only one set of footprints. He also noticed that it happened at the very lowest and saddest times in his life.

This really bothered him and he questioned the Lord about it. "Lord, you said that once I decided to follow you, you'd walk with me all of the way. But I have noticed that during the most troublesome times of my life, there is only one set of footprints. I don't understand why when I needed you most you would leave me."

The Lord replied, "My precious, precious child, I love you and I would never leave you. During your times of trial and suffering, when you see only one set of footprints, it was then that I carried you."[40]

Endnotes

[1] Charles Spurgeon, *Repentance after Conversion,* Sermon No. 2419, June 12, 1887.

[2] Robert R. Palmer, Bell I. Wiley, and William R. Keast, *The Procurement and Training of Ground Combat Troops* (Historical Division Department of the Army; First Edition 1948), pages 309-310.

[3] http://go.fold3.com/results.php?category=military&links=0&x-id=1515&s_kwcid=military%20service%20records

[4] http://www.skylighters.org/buzzbombs/index.html

[5] Stephen Ambrose, *Citizen of Soldiers: The U.S. Army from the Normandy Beaches to the Bulge to the Surrender of Germany* (Ambrose Tubbs, Inc., 1997).

[6] Michele Orzano, "Short Snorter" (*Coin World Magazine*, May 10, 2010).

[7] www.uboat.net/allies/merchants

[8] James Frank Alban, Jr., *My Army Book of Memories (published by Frank Alban, Jr., 2008-2011).*

[9] www.militaryhistoryonline.com/wwii/usarmy/artillery.aspx

[10] Rich Anderson, *US Army in World War II: Artillery and AA Artillery* (published by Rich Anderson, 2000).

[11] www.transchool.lee.army.mil/museum/transportation%20museum/redballintro

[12] www.transchool.lee.army.mil/museum/transportation%20museum/redballintro

[13] James Frank Alban, Jr., *My Army Book of Memories (*published by Frank Alban, Jr., http://143rdaaagunbnww2.com/, 2008-2011).

[14] James Frank Alban, Jr., *My Army Book of Memories (*published by Frank Alban Jr., http://143rdaaagunbnww2.com/, 2008-2011).

[15] en.wikipedia.org/wiki/Malmedy_massacre_trial

[16] *Antwerp X: The AAA War Against the Buzz Bombs*, originally published by men of the 50th AAA Brigade.

[17] www.longshoresoldiers.com/search/label/Antwerp

[18] www.longshoresoldiers.com/search/label/Antwerp

[19] www.longshoresoldiers.com/search/label/Antwerp

[20] John R. Bruning, *The Battle of the Bulge (*Zenith Press, 2011).

[21] John R. Bruning, *The Battle of the Bulge (*Zenith Press, 2011).

[22] www.longshoresoldiers.com/search/label/Antwerp

[23] www.archives.gov/nyc/exhibit/camp-kilmer

[24] www.efour4ever.com/mp40

[25] Christ Unlimited Ministries, "Wars and Rumors of War: What the Bible Says About War" (www.bibleresources.org/war)

[26] Michael Youssef, "My Journal" (published by Leading the Way, 2014), page 3.

[27] *War Cry: The Salvation Army Newsletter* (Volume 134, Number 5, 2014), page 10.

[28] Dr James Allan Francis, "The Real Jesus and Other Sermons"

(The Judson Press, Philadelphia: 1926), pages 123-124.

[29] *Final Flight (*Forrest McCullough Records, 1965).

[30] Christopher Snowbeck, "Mayor Blessed by North Side Church" *(Pittsburgh Post-Gazette,* Monday, January 10, 2000).

[31] Christopher Snowbeck, "Mayor Blessed by North Side Church" *(Pittsburgh Post-Gazette,* Monday, January 10, 2000).

[32] Douglas Heuck - Publisher/Editor, "Considering a Pittsburgh Tradition" (*Pittsburgh Quarterly*, Winter 2014), page 15.

[33] Melissa Pearce, "Bible Study on John 21:14" (*Faith Pittsburgh Magazine*, Spring 2014), page 23.

[34] Max Anders, *30 Days to Understanding the Bible* (Nashville: Thomas Nelson, 2004), page 135.

[35] C.S. Lewis, *Surprised by Joy* (New York: Harcourt, Brace and World), p. 226.

[36] Max Anders, *30 Days to Understanding the Bible* (Nashville: Thomas Nelson, 2004), page 135.

[37] www.gideons.org/AboutUs/OurHistory

[38] A. W. Tozer, *The Pursuit of God* (Camp Hill, PA: Christian Publications, 1997), page 102.

[39] http://www.wrensworld.com/clockoflife.htm

[40] Mary Stevenson, "Footprints in the Sand," from the original 1936 text

About the Author

Michael Peuler was born in Grand Rapids, Michigan to Christian parents. The oldest of six children, he loved sports and excelled in math and the sciences in school as a young boy. Michael enlisted in the U.S. Air Force and served a tour in Southeast Asia during the Vietnam War. Upon completion of his military obligation he graduated with honors from Grand Valley University in Allendale, Michigan with an accounting degree. Michael went on to become a Certified Public Accountant and a Certified Financial Planner and enjoyed a career in public accounting and banking. He has been a frequent speaker at banking schools and on television to discuss various financial topics. Michael currently serves as a financial consultant.

Michael has a heart for charity and travels to India to assist in the proclamation of Christ along with trips to Brazil and the Philippines for medical missions with Rotary International. Michael has served on numerous church, corporate and not-for-profit boards of directors. He loves to assist individuals with their finances.

Michael is married with two children and eight grandchildren and resides in western Pennsylvania with his wife, Victoria, whose father is the subject of this book.

How to Order Copies of Papa's Evangelistic Booklet

If you would like copies of the actual booklet Papa distributed, please note the prices below (U.S. Media Rate postage included):

10 copies	$ 5.50
25 copies	$11.00
50 copies	$16.50
100 copies	$27.50

Send requests along with checks payable to:

Michael Peuler
P.O. Box 2443
Cranberry Township, PA 16066

Allow 4-6 weeks for delivery (U.S. only)